Russia
IN THE WORLD ARMS TRADE

ANDREW J. PIERRE AND DMITRI V. TRENIN, EDITORS

CARNEGIE ENDOWMENT FOR INTERNATIONAL PEACE

© 1997 by the
Carnegie Endowment for International Peace
1779 Massachusetts Avenue, N.W.
Washington, D.C. 20036
Tel. (202) 483-7600
Fax. (202) 483-1840

To order *Russia in the World Arms Trade* ($14.95 paper),
contact Carnegie's distributor,
The Brookings Institution Press
Department 029, Washington, D.C. 20042-0029, USA.
Tel. 1-800-275-1447 or 202-797-6258
Fax. 202-797-6004.

Cover photos: Department of Defense (top left two photos);
 Agence France Presse (top right photo);
 AP/Wide World Photos (lower right).
Edited by Dixie T. Barlow.
Design by Paddy McLaughlin Concepts & Design.
Maps prepared by Dave Merrill.

Library of Congress Cataloging-in-Publication Data

Rossiia v mirovoi torgovle oruzhiem. English.
Russia in the world arms trade / Andrew J. Pierre and Dmitri V. Trenin,
editors.
p.   cm.
The book evolved from discussions of the Russian-American working group
convened by the co-editors in the fall of 1994 at the Moscow Center of the
Carnegie Endowment for International Peace.
Includes bibliographical references (p.   ).
ISBN 0-87003-083-3
1. Arms transfers—Russia (Federation)   2. Defense industries—Russia
(Federation) I. Pierre, Andrew J. II. Trenin, Dmitrii Vital'evich. III. Title.
HD9743.R92R6713 1997   97-31844
382'.456234'0947—dc21   CIP

Contents

Contents

Foreword to the English Edition

The future of Russia's arms industry, once the largest industrial sector of the Soviet Union's economy, remains highly uncertain and troubling. Russia's arms sales fell dramatically in the immediate post-Cold War years and are now increasing, albeit modestly. Many Russians perceive the West to be trying to squeeze them out of the world market—through the enlargement of NATO, for example, or through pressure to prevent arms sales to "rogue states." Westerners, for their part, are concerned about Moscow's controls—or lack thereof—over arms exports in general and about sales to particular countries, such as Iran and China.

Russia in the World Arms Trade, initially issued in Russian and the first book to be published on this subject in Russia since the end of the Cold War, is the result of a unique, two-year program of the Carnegie Moscow Center. Its chapters are based upon papers presented and discussions within the Russian-American Working Group on Conventional Arms Proliferation, headed by Andrew Pierre and Dmitri Trenin. The Working Group, as well as both the Russian- and English-language versions of this book, were made possible by generous support from the Carnegie Corporation of New York and the Starr Foundation.

The meetings of the Working Group brought together representatives of the various constituencies of the emerging Russian national security elite dealing with the defense industry and arms sales: government officials from a number of ministries, military and security officers, defense industrialists, politicians, academics, and members of the media. For many of these individuals, the Working Group provided a first opportunity to exchange views with their counterparts from the United States as well as Western European and other countries on arms transfer issues—a subject that in the Soviet period belonged among the most guarded state secrets. Indeed, for some of the Russian participants, this was also a first chance to openly discuss these issues with other knowledgeable Russian officials and military officers.

With the exception of one of the co-editors, Andrew Pierre, the authors are all Russians, and the book was prepared primarily for a Russian audience. We feel, however, that it is also of major interest to non-Russians who follow and study this issue—not least because of the authoritativeness of the contributors, who include a senior official from the Defense Council of the Russian Federation, a former deputy head of the Defense and Security Committee of the Russian Duma who now directs the Russian Institute of Strategic Studies, a senior Ministry of Foreign Affairs official, a leading journalist covering national security issues, a former defense industrialist now an authority on the industry, and several prominent academics.

Although the book also assesses the strategic and economic implications of Russia's arms sales, its primary emphasis is on the political dimension of the weapons trade. After the collapse of the Soviet Union, arms exports became a very sensitive issue in Russia—an issue symbolizing the decline, the dilemmas, and the opportunities of Russia on the world stage. *Russia in the World Arms Trade* places the subject within its Russian as well as its international context. For American readers, the book opens a window on an important and continuing Russian debate with significant implications for U.S. security interests around the world.

Jessica T. Mathews
President
Carnegie Endowment for
International Peace

About the Authors

Andrew J. Pierre, a former Senior Associate at the Carnegie Endowment for International Peace, is with the School of Advanced International Studies of Johns Hopkins University. He was previously Director-General of the Atlantic Institute for International Affairs in Paris and has held positions at the Council on Foreign Relations and Department of State. He is the author of *The Global Politics of Arms Sales* and editor of *Cascade of Arms: Managing Conventional Weapons Proliferation.*

Dmitri V. Trenin is Deputy Director of the Carnegie Moscow Center and Co-Chair of the Center's Foreign and Security Policy Project. He earlier taught at the Military Institute of the Military Academy of Economics, Finance, and Law and in 1993 became the first Russian military officer to be selected for the NATO Defense College. From 1993 to 1997, Dr. Trenin was a Senior Research Fellow at the Institute of Europe of the Russian Academy of Sciences. He has published numerous articles in both Western and Russian publications.

Pavel Felgengauer is defense correspondent for *Segodnya* newspaper. He has written numerous articles on Russian foreign and defense policy.

Mikhail I. Gerasev is Deputy Director of the Institute of the U.S.A. and Canada, Russian Academy of Sciences.

Sergei V. Kortunov is Deputy Chief of Staff of the National Security Council. From 1992 to 1994 he served as Chief of the Department of Arms Control in the Russian Ministry of Foreign Affairs.

Yevgeni M. Kozhokin is the Director of the Russian Institute of Strategic Studies. Formerly, he served as a member of Parliament and was Chairman of the Duma Subcommittee on International Security and Intelligence from 1990 through 1993.

Pyotr G. Litavrin is Chief of the Disarmament Section in the Ministry of Foreign Affairs. He was the Russian Federation's representative at the Group of Governmental Experts on the United Nations Register of Conventional Arms (1992-96).

Vitaly V. Naumkin is President of the Russian Center of Strategic and International Studies and Deputy-Director of the Institute of Oriental Studies of the Russian Academy of Sciences. He is the editor of *Central Asia and Transcaucasia: Ethnicity and Conflict* (1996).

Viktor M. Surikov is the Director-General of the Institute of Defense Studies (INOBIS). A recipient of the both the Lenin Prize and the U.S.S.R. State Prize, he is also a member of the Academy of Cosmonautics.

Acknowledgments

This book would not have been undertaken without the existence of the Carnegie Moscow Center—in many ways a unique locale for discussion and debate of international issues. We thank Morton Abramowitz, former President of the Endowment; Steven Sestanovich, former Vice President for Russian and Eurasian Affairs; and David Kramer, Melissa Eustace, and our other colleagues in Moscow and Washington for all of their assistance and encouragement. In particular, we thank Glenn Hodes, a Junior Fellow in Washington, for his many constructive ideas, substantive suggestions and knowledgeable clarification of the English-language text; and Ekaterina Stepanova for her assistance with arranging the meetings in Moscow and preparing the Russian-language text. We are also indebted to Valeriana Kallab for guiding the book to publication and Dixie T. Barlow for her editing.

The project on Conventional Arms Proliferation benefited from the suggestions of members of its advisory committee: Alexei Arbatov, Sergei Blagovolin, Steven Erlanger, Pavel Felgengauer, Sergei Karaganov, Alexander Konovalov, Sergei Kortunov, Yevgeni Kozhokin, Pyotr Litavrin, and Alexei Shulunov.

We would also like to warmly thank the authors and the commentators on the draft chapters, some of whom traveled from afar, and the participants in the Working Group, who are listed in the Appendix.

Chapter 1
Introduction

Andrew J. Pierre and Dmitri V. Trenin

In the fall of 1994, the Moscow Center of the Carnegie Endowment for International Peace convened a Russian-American Working Group on Conventional Arms Proliferation. Arms export issues had gained a special prominence in Russian political, social, economic, and even psychological spheres. Almost every political figure in the country had strong views on the subject. One could, however, discern a troubling consensus within Russia, particularly among those who had not had the opportunity to examine deeply what is known in Russia as the problem of international "military-technical cooperation."

From a purely economic standpoint, arms exports were viewed in Russia as the only way to bring the troubled military-industrial complex out of its crisis and to save national scientific and high-tech industrial potential. In the social sphere, the dwellers of the "closed cities"—scientists, engineers and workers of the military-industrial complex—were recognized as a powerful and well-organized interest group. Arms exports were also considered one of the most important political tools to promote Russia's influence in the world and to boost its international prestige. Psychologically, the rapid decline of Russian arms sales in the world market, concurrent with the disintegration of the U.S.S.R., was perceived as a consequence of ruthless attempts by the United States to squeeze out competitors from the market and achieve a position of dominance in the world arms trade. Thus, the very specific question of Russia's arms trade unexpectedly became a matter of everyone's concern and began to influence Russian foreign and defense policy as well as domestic policy in industrial and social domains.

The situation was complicated by the fact that the thick veil of secrecy that in the past had concealed information on Soviet

1

arms policies had now been replaced with a set of myths based on unscrupulous manipulations and selected facts. Apart from a narrow circle of professionals, very few people possessed an accurate knowledge of the main factors behind Russia's arms sales or developments in the world arms trade. Enthusiasts of exporting arms generated unrealistic expectations that were soon frustrated. The lack of a critical perspective on the experience of the Soviet Union in the international arms trade contributed to the myth that Russia had lost out on an enormous market.

On the American side, deep concern was raised over the collapse in Russia of controls over the nation's arms exports. America feared that advanced weapons could leak out of Russian armories and fall into unscrupulous hands. There was little confidence that the system of export controls in place during the Soviet era had been replaced by an equally effective one. Reports of the dire plight of the Russian defense industry and the ability of defense enterprises to sell their products directly to customers fed the belief that arms flows were getting out of hand. Many people, such as the late Mikhail Malei, President Yeltsin's one-time special advisor on defense conversion, declared that massive Russian arms sales were the only way to pay for defense conversion. This troubled the Americans, who feared that if Russia had difficulty competing for arms sales in the "open" markets, it would sell to countries to which the Western countries refused to sell. The potential transfer of arms to so-called "rogue" states—like Iran, Iraq, North Korea, and Libya—was seen in Washington as dangerous in terms of regional stability and peace.

The Carnegie Endowment's Russian-American Working Group comprised politicians, senior government officials, foreign diplomats stationed in Moscow, representatives of the military-industrial complex, high-ranking military figures, independent researchers and journalists (see list, p. 129). The participants earnestly attempted to provide an even-handed analysis of the entire complex of problems related to Russia's arms trade.

The group began its work by examining the patterns and trends of the global arms trade in the 1990s. The conventional wisdom in Russia at the time was that the United States had displaced Russia in the arms trade and was aggressively seeking large profits from an increase in its own sales. In this view, the

United States was seeking to monopolize the arms trade and prevent Russia from selling overseas—in effect, to squeeze Russia out of the market. A closer examination, however, revealed that while Russian arms sales were down dramatically, American arms sales had not increased in total amount. World arms sales had declined—as a fortunate by-product of the end of the Cold War and the easing of international tensions—yet American arms sales remained at an even level. Therefore, the American *proportion* of global arms sales had merely increased relative to the Russian proportion. This situation led to a great deal of misunderstanding and even suspicion. The Working Group faced the task of clarifying this situation.

The Working Group turned to the issue of Russian incentives for exporting military products and the obstacles hindering such exports. By the mid-1990s, Russian domestic defense arms and equipment procurement for its own forces fell to 20 percent of what it had been in 1991. Under these conditions, many in the group considered that a threshold had been passed and that the defense-industrial complex was beyond repair. Not only was the low volume of military manufacturing uneconomical, but defense enterprises were still maintaining a huge and unnecessary infrastructure. The technological capacities of subcontractors at the third and fourth tiers were disintegrating. Within a few years, Russia had lost a number of key industries including much of the electronics sector. Many experts believed that the top priority had to be the cessation of mass military production in an eleventh-hour attempt to save the basis of Russia's scientific and technological potential.

The group also felt that it was important to assess (against the background of the relevant American experience) to what extent arms exports were actually capable of preserving the Russian defense-industrial base and what their likely impact on defense conversion would be. Some felt that a Russian defense industry desperately struggling for survival had to forgo the uncertain path of conversion and instead attempt to expand arms exports.

A simplistic understanding of conversion is analogous to the belief that "a single touch can turn a sword into a ploughshare." A specific feature of conversion in Russia is that it coincides with large-scale economic transformation. While Russia ranks 10th in the world in terms of GDP and 75th in terms of GDP per capita, it remains among the world's top-ranking nations in terms of its defense expenditure.

Clearly, arms exports alone cannot compensate for evaporated domestic procurement. Moreover, the growing cost of Russian military products due to an escalation of Russian domestic prices vis-à-vis average world prices limited the profitability of exports. These problems are analyzed in great detail in Chapter 2, written by Mikhail Gerasev, Deputy Director of the Institute of the U.S.A. and Canada of the Russian Academy of Sciences, and Viktor Surikov, Director of the Institute of Defense Studies (INOBIS).

The next group of issues required an analysis of the fundamental principles of post–Cold War arms export policies. Now that the old ideological criteria are no longer relevant, what should the new guidelines look like? What could be the ideal mix of politics, economics, and ethics in this area? On what grounds could a country have its request for Russian or American arms rejected?

In an attempt to tackle these problems, the Working Group turned to the theory and practice of national controls over arms exports. An analysis of executive branch controls in Russia—Chapter 3 in this book—was prepared by Sergei Kortunov, a former senior official in the Ministry of Foreign Affairs charged with such issues, and subsequently a key advisor in the presidential administration of Boris Yeltsin. The proper role of the legislative branch was assessed in a contribution —Chapter 4 in this volume—by Yevgeni Kozhokin, a former deputy of the Russian Supreme Soviet and current Director of the Russian Institute of Strategic Studies. The following questions were asked: How does the new Russian export control system compare with similar systems in executive branches of the United States and the major European nations? What type of structure and relations between defense industries and the state would be optimal with the demise of the Soviet Union's mechanisms of the Military-Industrial Commission, Gosplan, and of the Communist Party Central Committee? Who are the real players in this field and who are the nominal ones, and how can they cooperate rather than play independent roles?

The group then turned to the role of the new legislative branch of government. What checks against abuses should be included in the law on military-technical cooperation? How broad can parliamentary prerogatives be in monitoring actions of executive authorities in the sphere that in Soviet days was mystically referred to as "special deliveries"?

The U.S. Congress plays a highly visible role in arms export control, through the adoption of appropriate legislation, the development of information through congressional hearings, and the lobbying by arms manufacturers and private interest groups (for instance, pro-Israeli or pro-Arab pressure groups). Congress is, however, limited to legislative oversight, rather than decision-making, on arms transfers. The role of the legislature in the control process in Britain, France, and Germany is minimal—essentially limited to cross-checks within the executive branch itself.

The Working Group also examined the complex issue of controlling exports of dual-use goods. How can legitimate dual-use transfers provide a boost to the Russian economy at the same time that appropriate export controls are ensured?

Arms sales obviously affect regional stability. The Working Group chose the Middle East/Persian Gulf and East Asia as two regions requiring more in-depth analysis. Presented in Chapters 5 and 6, these analyses were written by Vitaly Naumkin, an authority on the Middle East and currently president of the Russian Center of Strategic and International Studies, and by Pavel Felgengauer, one of the top defense analysts of the Russian media. These chapters consider effects of arms deliveries to Iran and China on the military balances in the respective regions and pay special attention to the question of whether economic benefits from arms exports outweigh political interests. They address the problems involved in the transfer of modern military technology to developing and newly industrialized nations, which could alter the global strategic landscape.

In this connection, it is important to find grounds for at least a limited system of arms trade regulation in the multi-polar world. Speaking at the U.N. General Assembly in September 1994, Russian President Boris Yeltsin suggested that international agreements in this field be concluded. Since the ranks of arms suppliers are limited, is it possible to reach agreement among them on mutual restraints in arms exports? What would be the criteria and procedure for limiting potentially destabilizing arms deliveries to certain countries? What could be the role of the new Wassenaar Arrangement, which has replaced COCOM? What should Russia's role be in shaping and maintaining the new international order in the field of arms transfers? How well do the existing mechanisms cope with their responsibilities? Which of them can be revived (for instance, the London Five-Party Talks in the context of a "small group" within the Wassenaar Arrangement)? Which of them need strengthening (e.g., U.N. Register of Conventional Arms)? Which should be set up anew (e.g., Russian-American bilateral consultations)? How realistic is agreement on a "code of conduct" in arms transfers, and would it be possible to observe its provisions in practice? These questions are considered in Chapter 7, written by Pyotr Litavrin, prominent Russian researcher and diplomat.

Competition in arms sales represents a new stumbling block in Russian-American relations. During the Cold War, Moscow and Washington armed their own clients. Today, Russia is fiercely fighting for markets in the Persian Gulf and Southeast Asia, while the United States may soon turn into the arms supplier of the former Warsaw Pact nations. Russia's military-technical cooperation with Iran, India, and China has become another source of discord between the United States and the Russian Federation. Is it possible to limit—if not prevent—the negative effect of such disputes on bilateral relations? Are Russian proposals to divide arms markets feasible or desirable, or is it impossible to preserve "traditional markets"? On the other hand, how far can international cooperation go, including Russian-American cooperation in developing, manufacturing, and marketing armaments? These problems are addressed in the final chapter, written by the co-chairmen of the Working Group, Andrew Pierre and Dmitri Trenin.

This book reflects Russian perceptions within governmental, industrial, and academic communities. It is noteworthy that the Carnegie Endowment's Conventional Arms Proliferation Project from the very beginning had the aim not of exposing or revealing previously unknown facts or classified data, as some feared, but rather of engaging in a serious dialogue on a highly complex and delicate problem where cooperation has always been second to competition. The Project did not confine itself to a dialogue between Russians and Americans. Discussion among various constituencies within Russia was equally important. Diplomatic contacts, official interdepartmental conferences, and parliamentary hearings notwithstanding, many politicians, government officials, industrialists and scientists, military experts, and journalists benefited—each in his or her own way—from informal contacts. The Russian-American Working Group at the Moscow Center of the Carnegie Endowment became a forum providing such contacts between 1994 and 1996. One of the important results of its activities is this book.

Chapter 2

The Crisis in the Russian Defense Industry: Implications for Arms Exports

Mikhail I. Gerasev and Viktor M. Surikov

The severe economic recession gripping Russia has especially affected the portion of Russian industry that once formed the backbone of the Soviet economy—the defense sector, including its scientific and technological potential. Between 1992 and 1995, production in the defense sector fell annually by 60 percent.[1] Many analysts believe that the very existence of the Russian defense industry, as well as the nation's high technology, is in jeopardy. This has wide implications, as the defense sector and its scientific and technological potential, along with the country's natural resources, remain the only assets on which to base the ultimate success of economic reform and the retention of Russia's status as an industrially developed nation.

This chapter is a study of the present crisis in the Russian defense industry and analyzes its principal causes and effects. It reviews the progress of defense conversion, placing special emphasis on an evaluation of the export potential of the Russian military-industrial complex and providing a critical assessment of the expectations concerning the export of arms.

The Russian Defense Industry— Yesterday and Today

One reason why the Russian defense industry's adjustment to new conditions has been so difficult is the fact that the military-industrial complex was always heavily supported and subsidized with financial resources, inventories, and research/technical personnel. On the threshold of the 1990s, the Soviet defense industry constituted an integral, multi-branch, organizationally independent complex. Within its framework, the Ministry of Defense (the customer) dealt with numerous defense factories through a complex bureaucracy that encompassed nine industrial ministries, special departments at the State Planning Committee (the Gosplan), the Military-Industrial Commission under the U.S.S.R. Council of Ministers, and the relevant departments at the Central Committee of the Communist Party of the Soviet Union. The defense sector was managed on the basis of a regimented array of documented forecasts and plans. These included Guidelines for the Development of Arms and Military Equipment, ten-year armament programs, and five- and one-year logistics plans. Thanks to a special price and tax system, the defense sector got eight times more value for its money than the commercial sector in its procurement of equipment.

This most-favored-sector treatment propelled the military-industrial complex to a leading position in the Soviet economy. Throughout this period, the defense industry determined the level of scientific and technological advancement and the pace of research and development for other sectors of the economy. A unique high-technology potential developed that throughout the postwar period enabled the Soviet Union to successfully compete with the defense industries of the United States and Western Europe. At one time the U.S.S.R. even overtook the United States as the largest supplier of arms to the world.

In the late 1980s, Soviet defense enterprises employed approximately 7.3 million people, including about 1.5 million people in research, design, development, and testing organizations. The cost of fixed production assets in the sector amounted to 108 billion rubles (at 1985 prices). Some factories, design organizations, and research centers had fixed production assets with a book value of more than 200 million rubles (at 1985 prices) and a workforce of 5,000 or more.[2]

Defense factories did not produce only arms and military equipment. They also manufactured virtually all household radio and television sets, sewing machines, and photographic and motion-picture equipment; some 97 percent of refrigerators; 70 percent of vacuum cleaners and washing machines; and 50 percent of all motorcycles manufactured in Russia. On the whole, defense factories produced a maximum of 22 percent of all consumer goods other than food (excluding output from light industry). Military items were also produced by electrical engineering or automobile factories, which were not technically part of the defense sector. Thus the parameters of the military-industrial complex were unclear—determined not so much by the fact that a given factory or an organization produced predominantly military products as by its respective affiliation with a particular ministry.

Following a general increase in consumer buying capacity after the institution of economic reforms in 1965, extensive manufacture of civilian goods in defense enterprises commenced. Over the Soviet Union's last fifteen to twenty years, the total share of civilian products as a percentage of overall defense factory output greatly swelled; by the early 1980s, it was at about 50 percent. This was quite remarkable, given the coterminous buildup of arms and military equipment (AME).[3] Facing continued confrontation with the West, arms production escalated.

Though conversion was not the order of the day, "diversification" of the defense sector was attempted through the establishment of factories geared toward development and manufacture of civilian products within a defense framework. In addition to consumer goods, the military-industrial complex produced large quantities of agricultural machines, tractors, cars, railway wagons, diesel engines, drilling and other oil and gas production equipment, medical instruments, civilian aircraft and ships, and other types of equipment for the national economy. At the start of the "acceleration and perestroika" policies in 1986-87, the defense sector led the drive to modernize light industry and the food industry. The declining level of military and political confrontation with the West and China was an impetus, as it reduced the requirements for arms and military equipment.

All of these efforts, however, had very limited results. Even though the defense industry was far ahead of the civilian sector in terms of its scientific, technological, and professional standards, a technology gap remained within the defense sector between its civilian and its military production.

* * *

In spite of, and probably in part as a result of, the defense sector's privileged status in the Soviet economy, all problems char-

11

acteristic of the larger economy were evident in the defense sector. The hallmark of the defense industry was a high degree of monopoly in arms and military equipment (AME) development and manufacture. As a result, the product assortment, R&D completion deadlines, and delivery amounts were frequently dictated by monopolistic factories proceeding from their own priorities. They tended to give preference to the development of more rugged and less research-intensive weaponry, which did not involve a high degree of technical risk, and they boosted the manufacture of costly military hardware at the expense of infrastructure upgrades. While formally remaining the customer, the Ministry of Defense was practically excluded from decision-making. The requirement that the armed forces be equally strong in all strategic aspects compounded the situation, but criticisms of this approach were smothered by the Communist Party and state discipline. These factors resulted in a heavy disproportion both in the defense sector itself and in the variety of AME produced. Firepower, for instance, was given priority, to the detriment of the upgrading of computer and C^3 (command, communication, and control) systems.

The defense industry handled assignments effectively, fulfilling orders on time and at an adequate scientific and technical level. However, the system lacked reliable mechanisms for raising the cost-effectiveness of R&D and manufacturing. Profitability of defense factories was of virtually no concern, which prompted heavy expenditure and an uncontrolled waste of limited resources on an ever increasing scale.

The material and human resources allocated for the development and manufacture of military equipment were generally shared among different industries rather than allocated efficiently to meet the needs of specific programs. This made for the excessive burgeoning of the defense sector. Bloated funding and a cumbersome and expensive system of decision-making on defense issues led to resource dissipation, duplicative R&D efforts, an unwarranted range of AME, and an unjustifiably large number of unique military production and research centers.

Following the breakup of the U.S.S.R. at the end of 1991, the Russian Federation inherited a defense sector consisting of 1,200 purely military-oriented factories with a workforce of some 4 million. Many more enterprises were partially engaged to fulfill defense orders. Together, they accounted for about 70-80 percent of the R&D potential and some 80 percent of the manufacturing capacity of the former Soviet military-industrial complex. Russia inherited the largest portion of factories producing artillery, firearms, aircraft, armored vehicles, and electronic warfare systems. However, Russia's opportunities to independently develop and produce even model arms and military equipment turned out to be limited because of the need for component supplies from other countries of the Commonwealth of Independent States (CIS). According to some estimates, for example, only a little over half of the basic models of attack weaponry can be autonomously produced by Russian factories. Regarding batch production of such equipment, the situation is even worse. Many factories that previously comprised part of a single AME production complex are now situated on the territories of other former Soviet republics. As a result, some AME models in 1992-1993 were manufactured thanks only to earlier-procured stockpiles or to limited deliveries under direct contracts between factories.[4]

After the breakup of the U.S.S.R. and the start of radical market reforms in Russia, the system of government defense orders collapsed. Official federal budget appropriations for purchases of AME shrank by 68 percent in 1992 (some data estimate the actual decrease between 80 and 90 percent).[5] As a result, output that year dwindled to one-third of that in 1991. The reduced acquisition of basic systems of armaments is illustrated in Table 1.

According to available information, in addition to the weapons systems listed in the table, munitions production plummeted by 93 percent, radio engineering products by 93 percent, and electronic products by 95 percent between 1992 and 1996.[6]

The dramatic decline in government contracts for AME resulted in drastic increases in the share of civilian output in "defense sector" operations. Today, the output share of military products in Russian defense factories frequently does not exceed 10 percent; numerous factories have discontinued the manufacture of such products altogether.[7] It should be noted, however, that factories in individual industries that are not organizationally part of the defense sector continue to produce military products as before.

Table 1

**Percentage Decreases in Arms and Military Equipment
(AME) Procurement, 1991 to 1992**

Weapons Systems	% Decrease
Intercontinental ballistic missiles (ICBMs)	55
Submarine-launched ballistic missiles (SLBMs)	39
Tactical missiles	81
Surface-to-air missiles	80
Air-to-air missiles	80
Aircraft	80
Tanks	97
Field artillery	97
Satellites and missile-delivery vehicles	34

Source: Ministry of Defense of the Russian Federation.

Because of conversion measures taken since the late 1980s, the drop in the manufacture of civilian products in the defense sector has proved substantially slower than in the industry as a whole. During the first quarter of 1992, for instance, civilian production in the military-industrial complex fell by only 7.7 percent compared to 13.5 percent in the industry as a whole. For 1993, the figures were 11 percent and 16 percent respectively. Nonetheless, the practical implementation of the Soviet conversion program laid the groundwork for a smoother transition of the defense sector to civilian output, despite conceptual errors and lack of due regard for the technological profile of specific companies during the planning of conversion targets.

By the beginning of 1994, however, the defense sector had exhausted its reserves, and the slump in both military and civilian output was far larger than in the average Russian industry. According to the Center of Economic Trends within the Government of the Russian Federation, the overall plunge in defense industry production during the first half of 1994 came to 37 percent, while civilian output in this sector decreased by 36 percent. These figures were greater than those for industry as a whole (26 percent).

One important overall feature of the decline is that the deepest cuts in civilian production occurred in precisely those defense industries where military orders were most reduced. Electronics industry factories experienced the steepest drops in AME output between the first half of 1993 and 1994 (57 percent), followed by the aircraft industry (56 percent), the communications industry (44 percent), and the arms industry (43 percent). The respective figure for the defense sector as a whole was 39 percent. The same industries reported the largest decreases (43 to 44 percent) in civilian output as well.

The decline in government contracts for AME has also had grievous social consequences. The exodus of qualified personnel from defense enterprises is on the increase. During the first half of 1994, the number of production staff in the defense sector diminished by 15 percent, up from 12 percent in 1993. This was due mostly to low wages, which did not exceed 70 percent of average pay in industry as a whole. The financial crisis in the country triggered a crisis of payment arrears, leaving defense factories in limbo. For example, in April 1994, the Defense Ministry's liabilities to armaments factories for shipped products came to 1.5 trillion rubles. Although the Ministry later managed to pay a significant portion of its liabilities to the defense complex, the system of settlements under government contracts remains disorderly, and payment defaults continue to be a chronic headache for companies in the sector. The conclusion is self-evident: The condition of the Russian defense sector is disastrous.

Conversion of Military Industry

The Soviet approach to defense conversion under President Mikhail Gorbachev was characterized by administration on command. Companies received directives as to which civilian goods instead of military ones they now had to produce. Such decisions disregarded the specialization and potential of specific factories and ignored the financial and social consequences of a transition from the logistically well-supported manufacture of military products to poorly organized and unprofitable civilian production.

Embarking on sweeping economic change on the threshold of 1992, Russian authorities adopted a different concept of conversion that emphasized economic rather than administrative leverage. The concept was based on the theoretically correct but oversimplified premise that shortages of manufactured goods were the principal drag on Russian economic development. This notion suggested that relieving plants of the burden of defense orders would not have any adverse effects at the macroeconomic level. On the contrary, it was believed this would make possible federal budget cuts and inflation control. One practical result of this policy change was a dramatic reduction in military spending and defense contracts.

The primary difference between the model of "economically driven conversion" and the Soviet model of "conversion by administrative command" lies in the fact that the government actually ignored the problem of filling the order books of enterprises in the military-industrial complex, leaving it up to the free-market environment and consumer initiative. The system of funding for the defense sector was likewise reshaped. Government defense contracts were cut to a minimum, and government orders for civilian goods were replaced with a system of subsidies and soft credits for converted defense factories.[8]

Although the policy seemed impeccable in theory, it disregarded a number of practical factors. First of all, it failed to take into account the dominant place of the military sector in the Soviet, and later Russian, economy. Drastic cuts in defense orders prompted a chain reaction of production cutbacks in virtually all branches of industry, including purely civilian ones. This in turn lowered federal budget revenues and increased the federal deficit.

Second, the emphasis on macroeconomics overshadowed problems within specific companies, such as the need to re-equip manufacturing facilities to make new civilian products for fresh markets, adapt defense factories to market conditions, and restructure production and management systems. Finding a solution to these problems required both additional time and substantial investment. But economic reform offered neither.

Third, the social aspects of across-the-board cuts in military production were virtually ignored. Social unrest in many ways was responsible for the failure to implement conversion in practice. The political undesirability of wholesale unemployment prevented the government of acting Prime Minister Yegor Gaidar in the early 1990s from taking the logical step of shutting down redundant production operations. As a result, mass "hidden" unemployment became prevalent, placing an extra financial and social burden on both the federal budget and the factories themselves.

Fourth, cuts in state defense orders coincided with the lifting of the government monopoly on foreign trade activities, which had been a fact of economic life for seven decades. Now, freedom to engage in foreign economic activities was declared. In theory, conditions should have been established for Russian businesses, including defense companies, to enter external markets and for factories in the military-industrial complex to launch manufacturing operations of high-tech civilian products that would be competitive in world markets. Such calculations were not realistic, however, because of fundamental differences between the military and the civilian product markets, the financial problems of companies, and the lack of free capital for investment.

Aspirations for international cooperation with the Russian military-industrial complex also failed to materialize. Three years after the commencement of reform, the finance share of foreign investors in defense modernization and conversion in Russia did not exceed a fraction of one percent of total funds spent for such purposes. At the same time, opening the Russian market to imports deprived defense factories of the possibility to survive by exploiting the vast potential of the domestic market with its enormous deferred demand. Domestic goods from the very outset proved unable to compete with imported products in terms of quality and then basically lost their last advantage of lower prices.

Finally, the emphasis on the entrepreneurial initiative of defense factories themselves, which was one of the key premises of the "economically driven conversion" concept, engendered yet another problem. Directors of defense factories had virtually no experience operating in market conditions, and they proved unable either to competently assess market trends or to make a calculated choice between development strategies. All of this resulted in duplicative efforts and domestic competition among companies in the military-industrial complex, many of which launched similar products on the market after failing to analyze actual demand. At the beginning of the 1990s, for instance, almost every major defense company offered its own model of a household washing machine, while twelve Russian factories simultaneously mastered the manufacture of oil pumping units. This nonsensical competition among Russian producers restrained the effectiveness of conversion efforts.

Together, the major problems described above demonstrate why the theoretically invulnerable concept of "economically driven conversion" has resulted in the progressive devastation of the Russian defense industry rather than in its conversion. Furthermore, this model has contributed to the real risk that Russia will rapidly lose its scientific and technological edge.

The mechanism of dismantling defense production operations is very simple. With defense orders down to a trickle, most factories in the military-industrial complex have idle manufacturing capacity of at least 40 percent. In conditions where prices on products manufactured under government contracts have a ceiling, this effective dead weight turns directly into unproductive overhead costs, further reducing the possibilities for a commercially viable operation in both military and civilian production. By the mid-1990s, most defense factories had overhead costs running to 900 percent or more, which completely nullified Russian industry's comparative advantages, such as relatively low costs for qualified manpower, raw materials, fuel, and power (all somewhat below world levels).[9]

Legal constraints on privatization of defense industries constituted yet another stumbling block. Their purpose was evidently to retain government control over the national defense sector and the mobilization potential of industry as a whole. But in present-day conditions these constraints have prevented defense factories from privatizing capacities that are in excess of defense needs. As a result, defense industries are unable to employ what has become the most popular method of short-term survival and production diversification in the Russian economy during the first half of the 1990s.

In conclusion, the Russian defense industry finds itself in a precarious situation. It cannot be competitive in either external or domestic markets; it cannot stay afloat because of a lack of government contracts; and it cannot undergo restructuring because of the absence of investment resources as well as the conditions in which the military-industrial complex was placed by the state privatization program.

Arms Exports: Panacea or Imperative for Survival?

The concept of military-technical cooperation (MTC) as used in Russia and the former Soviet Union encompasses not only exports and imports of arms and military equipment, but also the provision of military-technical services, free or preferential aid, manufacturing licenses, cooperation with other nations in the development of arms and military equipment, and more.

In the Soviet Union, the choice of MTC partners and forms of cooperation was determined almost exclusively by political and strategic considerations in the context of global confrontation between the superpowers. Economic profit was of secondary significance and was disregarded in most cases. Furthermore, the existence of a mammoth domestic market for AME reduced the economic incentive for foreign military-technical cooperation. As a result, the MTC factor was not taken into account either during the strategic planning phase or during the stages of development and mass production of armaments.

The most significant economic incentives for MTC include:

1. Hard currency proceeds and a positive impact on the balance of payments.
2. Reduced domestic arms procurement costs with "economies of scale" in production.
3. Sustained employment and the maintenance of defense-industrial infrastructure.
4. Reductions in R&D costs for mass-produced arms.
5. Military production spin-offs to catalyze other economic, scientific, and technological development.

19

Now that Russia's economic, political, and strategic situation has dramatically changed, the government's approach to MTC has refocused almost exclusively on economic interests. Current discussions within Russian political circles on MTC policies still almost exclusively feature arguments for maximizing foreign exchange receipts. Advocates of exploiting MTC to this end speak of drastically improving Russia's foreign trade balance by exporting AME and using extra profits to bankroll the conversion of defense industry. They argue that in the middle of the 1980s, Soviet AME exports topped $18 billion. The potential of Russian AME exports is estimated by some experts to be $10-$15 billion per year. According to conventional wisdom: The people have invested in the development of the defense industry for decades, and finally the time has come for it to pay its dues.

The continuing contraction of the world AME market casts doubt on such overly optimistic estimates of Russian export possibilities. Even if Russia regains the market share previously held by the Soviet Union, AME sales might grow to around $7 billion at best. Even if fully received in cash (which is highly unlikely), this amount would be too insignificant to make a decisive impact on the country's foreign trade balance. It would certainly not resolve the problem of sufficient funding for conversion of the military-industrial complex, estimated by some analysts to require $150 billion.[10]

The prevalent perception that military-technical cooperation is a cure-all for all economic ills is not only fallacious but also myopic. The emphasis on deriving maximum currency proceeds makes it necessary to demand payment for AME in cash, or at least on a barter basis. Deliveries on credit, especially on preferential terms, are seen as running counter to national interests. This approach, however, considerably limits the range of potential customers, thereby narrowing market opportunities and forestalling other economic advantages to military-technical cooperation described above.

The prevailing view that the defense industry is an export-oriented sector neglects the reality that, regardless of changes in the international situation, the nation's top priority remains maintaining Russia's defense capacity and protecting its citizens. The development of military equipment by the defense sector primarily serves these purposes—despite its extra burden on the national economy. The objective of a rational government policy should be to alleviate this burden in any way possible, but not to the detriment of defense capability. For example, the government should encourage scientific and technological spin-offs from the military-industrial complex to civilian purposes and should actively promote MTC with other countries as a way of assisting the defense industry.

Savings resulting from mass production and the maintenance of both employment and infrastructure are important aims underlying the government's motivation to export arms. Steep reductions in domestic arms procurement and manufacture represent an additional impetus. Since the early 1990s, production of basic types of arms and military equipment for the Russian armed forces has been decreasing to levels comparable to that of second-tier arms exporters like the United Kingdom, France, and Germany throughout the 1970s and 1980s.

The defense industries of these three countries depend heavily on exports. During the 1980s, France, the United Kingdom, and West Germany exported an average of 50 percent (in value) of all their AME production. Even more illustrative are data revealing the dependency of individual defense firms on exports. In the 1980s, for example, the export share in total military-oriented output of French companies like Thompson, Aerospaciale, Dassault, and Matra ranged between 50 percent and 75 percent.[11]

In theoretical terms, the need for exports is determined by the known ratio between the cost of an equipment prototype and its serial manufacture. Western experts estimate that increasing serial production from 400 to 800 aircraft decreases the unit cost by 15 percent, and an additional increase in output to 1,200 aircraft would yield savings of 28 percent. In such cases, exports become an indispensable condition to fulfill national armament programs. For instance, the commercially profitable production and, accordingly, the acceptable level of purchasing prices on French Mirage fighters requires export levels of at least 25 percent; the respective figure for Swedish Grippen fighters is 30 percent. Unit costs of the German Leopard tank have been reduced by 57 percent through exports.[12] Northrop, the leading U.S. contractor for the B-2 bomber program, offered to trim the price of each aircraft from $850 million to $595 million if the Pentagon doubled its original request for twenty bombers.

This all serves to illustrate a central point. The armed forces of a country experiencing sharp reductions in defense appropriations, forced cutbacks, and retrenched AME production has a limited range of strategic options. It may:

- Refrain from maintaining adequate qualitative levels in military equipment;
- Rely on imports to meet its modernization requirements;
- Continue reduced production of AME for domestic defense needs in small amounts, facing dramatically increased unit costs; or
- Rely on exports to sustain the efficiency of the defense industry and to lower domestic defense procurement costs.

Like the other arms manufacturers of the world, Russia views vigorous export policies as the only solution. When exports do not represent "the solution," a country as a rule is compelled to incur additional expenditures in order to complete declared arms programs. Former French Defense Minister François Leotard made the revealing admission when he acknowledged that, from a strictly financial standpoint, France should have bought U.S. Hercules military transport aircraft instead of pursuing domestic production. The Ministry of Defense rejected the less costly option because the manufacturing program was too important to French industry.[13]

One can conclude that essential cuts in the Russian armed forces and the steep reduction in their requirement for AME compel a no less objective need to promote the sale of Russian military equipment abroad. The country's interest in the success of this policy proves to be even greater than the interest of individual producers. Exports are a key prerequisite for lessening the economic burden of military spending and ensuring the efficiency of defense industries as the core of Russia's defense potential.

An economic perspective on MTC policy suggests some specific approaches. Extending weapons on credit or on preferential terms, which has been denounced in recent years, no longer looks harmful, since losses in foreign trade turnover can be largely compensated by savings, thanks to increased production lots and, consequently, reduced domestic expenses for arms procurement. Additionally, the current principle of "payment in cash during the year of delivery" sharply limits potential customers for Russian AME, preventing long-term gains through supplies of spare parts, components, and such.

While noting the importance of MTC as a tool to fulfill the above tasks, one should admit that in present-day conditions, AME exports alone cannot provide the "magic" solution to problems in the Russian defense industry. While Russia's situation is unique, both in terms of the extent and pace of cuts in the defense budget and in past military-oriented production, all of the world's major AME producers, including the United States, are experiencing similar problems. The reaction of most AME manufacturing countries to changes in both the domestic and international markets is indicated by the gathering momentum to restructure their industries. A number of large AME manufacturing companies have merged, strategic alliances have been forged, production has become concentrated, and excess factories have closed.

A radical regrouping of forces in Western defense industries is under way. In the United States, for instance, General Dynamics in 1993-94 announced the sale of its tactical aviation division to Lockheed, its guided missile division to Hughes, and its electronic systems division to Carlyle. Northrop bought Grumman. Lockheed and Martin-Marietta consolidated. Similar trends are evident in Europe, where talks are under way between British Aerospace and France's Matra as well as between France's Aerospaciale and Germany's DASA. These examples are just the tip of the iceberg; even more dynamic developments are occurring at the level of small and medium-size defense subcontractor firms. According to some experts, up to eighty defense companies will have ceased to exist by the end of this decade. In the opinion of the head of British Aerospace, there will be only one major manufacturer of military aerospace equipment left in Europe within the next few years.[14] The results of this restructuring and concentration of forces in the immediate future will be to adjust the output of military-industrial complexes in Western countries to match changes in domestic demand. Further cost-cutting and growing efficiency could result in increased competitiveness by Western countries in the global arms market.

In Russia, where the decline in defense appropriations has been unprecedented and the redundancy of military production operations is much higher than in the West (around 60 percent), restructuring the defense sector is both urgent and vital. Steps to establish Russian "finance-and-industry groupings" must be viewed as only the first step in this direction. Restructuring the defense sector is an ambitious task that can only be fulfilled if based on clear-cut priorities for industrial and military-technical development established by the state. The growth of a new system would enable radical cuts in excess capabilities, providing surviving factories with enough government orders to remain profitable.

Nevertheless, the strategies suggested here to manage problems facing the Russian defense-industrial complex involve considerable social costs, including an upsurge in unemployment. But today's "hidden" joblessness in the defense sector may present no less of a danger or burden for the national economy. Attempts to apportion domestic defense orders among many plants ultimately threaten to destroy the entire Russian defense industry. The expectation that Russia's military-technical cooperation with other countries will solve all of the problems in the defense sector is not only naive, but also extremely dangerous, as it has postponed tough decisions. With strong government backing, AME can become a key factor for maintaining economically sound industries in Russia, but only after industries are radically curtailed and consolidated. Otherwise, even the most extensive sales will not be able to save the domestic defense sector from a total collapse in the future.

Notes

[1] Gen. A. A. Sitnov, head of the Russian armed forces' armaments program, as quoted by *Krasnaya Zvezda*, July 15, 1995.

[2] Military-Industrial Commission under the U.S.S.R. Council of Ministers (1989).

[3] *Industrial Policy Concept in the Russian Defense Industry*. Committee of the Russian Federation for Defense Industries. Central Research Institute for the Economics and Conversion of Military Production, Moscow, 1993, 5.

[4] This was acknowledged by the First Deputy Minister of Defense of the Russian Federation Andrei Kokoshin at a meeting in the Ministry of Defense.

[5] *Obshchaya Gazeta*, July 1-7, 1994.

[6]Source: Alexei Shulunov, chairman of the League of Assistance to Defense Enterprises.

[7]Since the start of 1994 alone, more than seventy factories in the defense sector have completely stopped any manufacture of military products. (*Segodnya*, September 30, 1994)

[8]*Industrial Policy Concept in the Russian Defense Industry*, 6.

[9]Based on authors' interviews with defense factory managers.

[10]*Segodnya*, October 18, 1994.

[11]Stockholm International Peace Research Institute. *SIPRI Yearbook, 1990.* Oxford University Press, London, 326-328.

[12]Keith Kraus. *Arms and the State: Pattern of Military Production and Trade*, Cambridge University Press, 1992, 141.

[13]*Finansoviye Izvestia*, May 26–June 1, 1994.

[14]*Finansoviye Izvestia*, September 8–14, 1994.

Chapter 3

Arms Export Controls: Competition Among Executive Agencies

Sergei V. Kortunov

In the Soviet Union, an effective state system of arms export control existed within the executive branch in the context of a state command economy. This system functioned on the premise of seeking to prevent damage to the military, economic, and strategic interests of the U.S.S.R. It was based on a number of decrees and other enactments that took into account the international commitments of the Soviet Union and was characterized by strict secrecy and a state monopoly over all foreign economic activity.

Apart from the centralized economy, another factor that rendered the arms export control system in these years highly effective was the U.S.S.R.'s penchant to supply arms primarily on political and ideological grounds, often on a barter basis, and sometimes free of charge. As a superpower, it tried to confront the United States in all regions of the world through arms transfers to its clients. The relative economic isolation of the Soviet Union also contributed to the effectiveness of the export control system.

After the breakup of the U.S.S.R. in 1991, the Soviet export control system ceased to exist. At the same time, Russia's transition to a market economy was accompanied at the international level by a shift from the isolationist model to a large-scale integration of global economics. The breakup of the U.S.S.R. also spelled the decline of ideology in the entire post-Soviet space. Taken together, these factors influenced the way the arms trade was managed and controlled.

A struggle among the different agencies of military-technical cooperation (MTC) for the right to trade arms, on the one hand, and the right to supervise and profit from this trade, on the other, led to permanent changes in the Russian system of MTC and resulted in the absence of a national consensus on these issues. Understandably this "reorganization" has created confusion in both domestic and foreign political circles. One should bear in mind, however, that this state of affairs is quite logical and reflects the transitional nature of Russia's current experience.

Shaping a National System of Export Control at a Time of Market Transition

In 1991, each new or potential player in military-technical cooperation was confident that it could manage arms sales independently, without professional assistance. State foreign economic companies Oboronexport and Spetsvneshtechnika (formerly the Main Engineering and the Main Technical departments) each held the legal status of independent entities to license arms transfers. Both of these autonomous agencies were under the Ministry of Foreign Economic Relations. Some military-aircraft industry enterprises, unhappy with the sluggishness of the old structures of this Ministry, and their inability to efficiently promote Russian arms in the world market, also started to seek the right of independent access to external markets. The State Committee for Defense Industries, Goskomoboronprom, claimed to speak for all weapons producers and tried to get its share of the market as well.

The direct contact and access by defense enterprises to foreign partners, authorized since 1991, was intended to enhance the effectiveness and profitability of arms transfers and also to discourage manufacturers from turning to various "brokers." Directors of defense enterprises declared themselves ready to negotiate independently with potential foreign buyers. It seemed that the transformation of arms production into a more commercial activity gave producers the opportunity to derive substantial benefits. This was quite unlike past experiences, when all of the profits from the state-centralized, state-financed defense industry were absorbed by the federal budget.

Facing a drastic decline in state orders and the failure of defense conversion, defense enterprises found themselves in a critical position. They strove hard to export military equipment. Beyond the factory directors there were collectives of thousands of workers that could fall apart without exports, resulting in the loss of unique technologies and product designs.

Political crisis, administrative chaos, and the transition to a market economy in 1991-92 objectively weakened the state's control over foreign economic activity. The move to republic and even regional sovereignty within the Russian Federation contributed to the almost uncontrolled export of non-ferrous metals, valuable strategic materials, and technologies. Enterprises entitled to seek buyers independently often tried to sell directly as well. In a number of cases, this included entire defense enterprises.

What happened was that a lack of trading skills resulted in chaos, in rapidly negotiated contracts for arms sales on clearly unfavorable terms, and in the loss of potential markets. In some instances, arms were offered to customers at prices below production costs. In other cases, because of the absence of any coordination among manufacturers, various enterprises simultaneously entered the markets of certain countries (e.g., Malaysia), thus threatening the entire breadth of military-technical cooperation with those countries.

Russia's entry into new and untested markets and fierce competition with other countries required better support and coordination on the part of the state. Currency credits were needed immediately to support a number of unique technologies and manufacturers, and the state could not provide them. In addition, Russian firms were demanding "payment in hard currency during the year of delivery," despite the fact that this had long ago been abandoned in the world arms trade, where almost all arms deals are now made on credit.

Guidelines to regulate Russian arms exports and transfers of sensitive technologies were slow to develop in 1991-92. Military-technical cooperation was advancing on an inadequate legal base, with incompatible administrative and regulatory acts. These acts were, however, conducive to settling troublesome situations regarding conventional arms export control (and in a broader sense, over MTC) and to preventing arms sales unauthorized by the state.

On February 22, 1992, President Boris Yeltsin signed the Decree On the Types of Products Prohibited for Unauthorized Sale, stipulating obligatory licensing of arms, military equipment, and other special assets. A year later, on January 28, 1993, a decree of the Council of Ministers endorsed the list of military products, the export and import of which was licensed. Subsequently the Law on Military-Technical Cooperation of Russia with Foreign States was drafted along with the Concept of Military-Technical Cooperation with Foreign States. While both documents were submitted for consideration to the Parliament, neither was enacted during Yeltsin's first presidential term. Another administrative tool of arms export control attempted was the establishment of a single system of decision-making, licensing, and customs control. This system took into account Russia's foreign policy priorities, the transition to a market economy, and international standards in export controls.

Under the Presidential Decree of May 12, 1992, in order to provide for a single state policy on arms sales and to coordinate these efforts, the Interdepartmental Commission for Military-Technical Cooperation of the Russian Federation with Foreign States was established. Furthermore, a statute on Military-Technical Cooperation of Russia with Foreign States, stipulating the procedure for state regulation of defense exports and imports, works, and services in the field of military cooperation, was adopted as a temporary substitute for legislation.

Lessons from the experiences of major Western exporting states in securing effective control over arms sales would be valuable in shaping a comparable system in Russia. Alongside the formulation of a national system of export controls, a process of establishing contacts and enhancing dialogue between Russia and the West started in 1992-93 so that harmony in conventional arms control mechanisms might be reached in the future. The 1996 Wassenaar Arrangement—an international mechanism on export controls and non-proliferation (and the successor to COCOM)—will play a vital role in this respect. Conventional arms control is one of the few realms still lacking international legal regulations as well as established mechanisms of multilateral negotiation and consultation.

Russia's main international commitments to conventional arms export control stem from the Guiding Principles for

Conventional Arms Sales. The Principles were first elaborated within the framework of consultations among the five permanent members of the U.N. Security Council—the United Kingdom, the United States, France, Russia, and China—who also happened to be the five leading arms exporting countries at the time. This 1992 document established criteria for the legitimacy of a specific transfer. In accordance with the Guiding Principles, the five countries (the P-5) agreed to refrain from arms transfers that could:

- Protract or aggravate existing armed conflict;
- Increase regional tensions;
- Introduce a destabilizing military potential into the region;
- Violate any embargo or other internationally agreed limitations;
- Be used for purposes other than the need for a recipient state's legitimate defense;
- Support international terrorism; or
- Undermine the national economy of the importing state.

Russian arms transfer decision-making takes into account the resolutions of international organizations, first and foremost the United Nations, concerning prohibitions on specific states. Russia also complies with U.N. resolutions on international transparency in arms transfers. Among the countries currently subject to an embargo on arms sales are Iraq, the republics of the former Yugoslavia, and Libya. The Ministry of Foreign Affairs of the Russian Federation monitors international commitments of this kind.

Thus an export control regime that takes into account the military, political, and economic interests of Russia has been in the making since 1992. It has been shaped and improved in light of international control mechanisms as well as the experiences of the main exporters of arms and military equipment.

The Impact of Global Competition and State Protectionism on Russia's Export Policies

The export control system of the executive branch evolved in a perplexing international context that influenced this process both directly and indirectly. It is well known that from 1990 to 1993 the U.S.S.R. and later Russia faced a drastic decline

31

in the aggregate volume of arms exports. There were objective and subjective reasons for this. After the Cold War ended, competition among leading arms exporters became more pronounced, catching Russia off-guard. Underlying harsh competition was a new reality that the end of East-West confrontation engendered a drastic decline in demand for arms in the so-called Euro-Atlantic space. This was a strong blow for the leading Western military-industrial companies. The governments of all major arms exporting countries, including Russia, were strongly pressured by their national military-industrial complexes to enact state protectionist policies. One vehicle for such a policy was the active promotion of products at arms exhibitions. Defense firms in the United States, the United Kingdom, and France benefited from state assistance. One only has to recall the efforts of U.S. President George Bush and Secretary of State James Baker to promote the sale of 150 F-16 aircraft to Taiwan, or the similar activities of French President François Mitterand to promote the sale of sixty Mirage fighters to the same country. The implementation of the 1990 Conventional Forces in Europe Treaty (CFE), moreover, led to deep cuts in conventional arms and resulted in a drastic decline of purchases in participating states.

At the same time, the end of the Cold War has contributed to increased tension and the revival of national ambitions in various regions of the world. As a result, demand for new arms has increased markedly in Southeast Asia, Africa, and the Middle East. Moreover, the Gulf War demonstrated to Third World countries the benefits of having state-of-the-art weaponry in their inventories. Every country, including clients of the former U.S.S.R., faced the task of modernizing its armed forces. This, in turn, generated the belief among developed arms-producing countries that the world arms market, so stratified during the Cold War and declining for some years, had suddenly opened up, revealing "empty spaces" of fresh opportunities for the export of arms.

Failure of Talks Among the Five

As a consequence of the factors mentioned, the five main arms-exporting countries, no longer constrained by the political or ideological considerations of the past, started an unprecedented rivalry for old and new markets. The economic interests of the military-industrial complexes of arms exporting countries shifted to the forefront of world politics.

Thus, it was not by mere chance that the talks of the P-5 were suspended in 1992. At that point the notion of control mechanisms and arms trade limitations was discarded. The notorious deal between the United States and Taiwan for 150 F-16 aircraft presented China with a long-awaited pretext to withdraw from the talks. For the United States, too, the opportunity of unhampered transfers started to prevail over the desire to formulate a mutually acceptable code of conduct on arms trade. Having undermined its own proposal for "advance notifications" of arms sales—most likely, the United States tried to impose this procedure on the Five to enhance its leverage in competition with the other exporters—the Americans eventually lost interest in the talks.

As a result, the London Guiding Principles, elaborated with great pains in 1991-92, were sacrificed—and not even to long-term political interests, but to immediate economic gains. France was content with China's withdrawal from the P-5 talks and was particularly happy that the blame for their suspension fell on the United States. Just several months later, Taiwan's order from France of sixty Mirage aircraft was announced. After China indicated its readiness to resume participation in the work of the Five under a new format (as a result of Russia's mediation effort), France used various pretexts to renounce a revival of the forum, despite earlier agreements.

A Clash of Interests in the Field of Export Control

Given the predominant role of the military-industrial complex in Russia's economy, the end of the Cold War had great consequences. In 1992 alone, military production in Russia shrank by 60 percent. Drastic cuts in state arms procurement resulted in the closure of entire factories. The enormous work force of the military-industrial complex had been a mainstay of the regime and had always enjoyed a privileged status in the Soviet Union. With the loss of this status, it turned into a latent source of social instability. The Russian government had to address this problem and, following the precedents of the major Western countries, enacted policies providing protection for national arms manufacturers. Yet, unlike these countries, Russia implemented protectionist policies in an incompetent and inefficient manner.

This trend influenced Russia's national system of arms export control. The system was shaped in 1992-95 against the background of a harsh struggle among various groups in government, first of all between the "state-minded" (advocates of a strict state control on arms exports) and the "market-minded" (those favoring a maximum liberal regime according broad rights to the manufacturers). The state-minded view was traditionally shared by the Ministry of Foreign Affairs, the Ministry of Foreign Economic Relations, the Foreign Intelligence Service, and the Ministry of Defense. The market-minded view corresponded more to military factories and to the State Committee for Defense Industries, Goskomoboronprom (since 1996, Ministry for Defense Industries, or Minoboronprom), which claimed to speak for defense enterprises—although this claim was not always supported by the enterprises themselves.

This struggle continues today with varying degrees of success on both sides, conditioning a ceaseless redressing of the national system of export controls. It also results from Russia's entry into heretcfore unfamiliar export markets, such as Southeast Asia or the Persian Gulf. A clash of interests reflects Russia's search for an optimal and delicate balance between the "free rules" of a market economy and the rigid control regulations of executive bodies of government. While this problem has been effectively tackled in Western countries, Russia has just begun to seek such a balance.

As for policy, this clash of interests reflects the quest for a different although no less delicate balance: namely, that between strategic interests and purely economic or commercial interests. What is of greater importance in an arms sale—earning hard currency or involving another country in one's sphere of political influence? Once again, Western arms exporting countries have addressed this problem, while Russia has just started to seek a solution. This delay is due partly to the fact that Russia has yet to clearly define its national interests and national identity. The absence of a valid concept of national security[1] precludes Russia from solving the problem, which engenders a kind of dilemma: Russia must win international arms contracts for the welfare of domestic industry, but at the same time as it must limit the export of high-tech weaponry and products for reasons of national security.

In the Soviet Union, political considerations were always given priority over commercial benefit in arms sales. For decades, the Soviet military-industrial complex received guarantees of payment from the state, while a large fraction of equipment that did not go into service in the Soviet army was sold on preferential terms or delivered free of charge to friendly regimes as a political reward. The only exceptions were Iraq and Libya, which provided hard currency returns; however, after embargoes were placed on them, the debt of these countries, too, increased.

Soviet President Mikhail Gorbachev undertook the first attempt to re-orient military-technical cooperation on a commercial basis by granting a maximum degree of freedom to manufacturers. This period can be thought of as "market romanticism"; its guiding principle was "sell to anyone who pays"—aside from countries subject to U.N. sanctions or those openly hostile to the U.S.S.R. However, it soon became clear that "payment in cash during the year of delivery" was a principle that could not apply under the crisis situation in the defense industry, given its uncompetitiveness and lack of substantial experience in new markets. Currency revenues from arms sales plummeted. A state policy designed to channel revenues from arms sales toward defense conversion failed.

Meanwhile, the state monopoly on arms trade weakened substantially. It goes without saying that the conditions of the modern market require the certification of products, a reliable after-sale service, and supplies of spare parts. Unfortunately, this has always been the Achilles heel of the Soviet and later Russian arms exports. For decades, transfers relied on barter deals with developing countries content with minimal after-sale servicing. As testified by the experience of earlier conflicts in the Middle East as well as by the Persian Gulf War, sophisticated weapons were often exported to countries having little idea how to operate them effectively.

Apart from manufacturing high-quality military equipment, an exporter has to be good at managing sales follow-ons and securing its reliable maintenance operation. The Russian producers could not orient themselves quickly to that need; it had always been a Soviet weakness. For instance, while market trends for Russian high-tech equipment are currently unfavorable, the demand for spare parts is strong. In many countries, Russian aircraft such as the MiG-21 and MiG-23 still operate, requiring service, maintenance, and modernization. Russian manufacturers have obviously underestimated the opportunities in this promising market, and now it is being taken over by Western manufacturers ready to modernize Soviet military hardware.

The failures of Russian arms enterprises in the world market did not discourage further activity. In 1993-94 they continued to seek independence from complete state control, acting both independently and through Goskomoboronprom.

In May 1994 the Government of the Russian Federation endorsed a special Statute on Certification and Registration of the Right of Enterprises to Export Arms, Military Equipment, and Works and Services for Military Needs. Certified and registered enterprises that developed and manufactured arms or military equipment were now entitled to: seek foreign clients in countries with which military-technical cooperation was not prohibited, exhibit arms and military equipment cleared for export, disclose tactical and technical specifications during talks, quote an approximate price that had been duly agreed, and carry out marketing. Above all, they could independently sign contracts and export arms, military equipment, and works and services produced in excess of state defense orders on the basis of duly obtained licenses.

According to the Statute, certification was to be made by the Interdepartmental Commission for Military-Technical Cooperation of the Russian Federation with Foreign States upon the request of Goskomoboronprom, the State Committee for Defense Industries. Goskomoboronprom required an application with a requisite set of documents and could conduct an on-site inspection of the enterprise. Copies of the application with the documentation kit were forwarded to the Ministry of Foreign Economic Relations, the Ministry of Defense, the Federal Counterintelligence Service, the Ministry of the Economy, the State Customs Committee, and the State Company Rosvooruzheniye. The application itself was considered by the

Certification Commission of Goskomoboronprom, which included representatives of these same agencies. The recommendations of Goskomoboronprom were generally approved. The agencies that could professionally assess the political consequences of a deal, in particular the Ministry of Foreign Affairs, were involved in decision-making only at its final stages.

Recent Trends

The victory of "the market minded" over "the state minded" in the field of military-technical cooperation set by the May 1994 Statute was only a temporary one. It immediately became clear that implementation of this act would conflict with the interests of the powerful State Company Rosvooruzheniye, which was created by presidential decree in November 1993 to manage arms export and import. This company was modeled on and became the successor of the Association Oboronexport, the State Foreign Trade Company Spetsvneshtechnika, and the Main Department for Collaboration and Cooperation of the Ministry of Foreign Economic Relations. According to the decree, arms export is centralized and can be effected only on authorization of Rosvooruzheniye, which issues licenses for military-technical cooperation. Rosvooruzheniye was charged with investing private and state capital into the enterprises of the Russian military-industrial complex with a view to contractual manufacture of arms enjoying the highest demand on the world market. A post of Special Representative of the President of the Russian Federation was set up within Rosvooruzheniye (occupied until 1996 by Marshal Yevgeni I. Shaposhnikov, and then abolished). In autumn 1994, President Yeltsin made yet another move to strengthen presidential control over arms exports by establishing the post of Special Adviser on issues of military-technical cooperation.

Finally, on December 30, 1994, the President signed a decree creating the State Committee of the Russian Federation on Military-Technical Policy, directly accountable to the head of state (Sergei I. Svechnikov was appointed acting chairman of the committee). The State Committee was charged with:

- Drafting and implementing state policy in the field of military-technical cooperation of the Russian Federation with foreign countries;

- Elaborating draft laws on state policy in the field of MTC and military industry pertinent to the competence of the Committee;
- Coordinating activities among federal bodies of the executive to implement armament programs, defense conversion, and limitation or disposal of arms and military equipment;
- Regulating and coordinating the activities of participants' military-technical cooperation; and
- Supervising foreign economic activity related to military-technical cooperation.

For the first time, a single state body undertook all of these functions. The State Committee was to partake in drafting federal programs on and conceptual approaches to MTC, projects under respective intergovernmental accords, and programs with foreign countries to cooperatively develop and manufacture arms and military equipment; it was also to participate in the work of state commissions and international organizations. Additionally, the Committee was charged with licensing MTC projects and elaborating the state defense order on defense exports. It prepared and managed the export part of the state defense order and participated in the settlement of Russia's external debt and foreign debts owed to Russia. It was essential that the Committee supervise Russian compliance with international treaties on military-technical cooperation. It was also to control the receipt and use of currency proceeds from export operations, which entailed supervising credits to importer-states and their receipt and repayment.

The new agency coordinated R&D planning to support and develop the export potential of defense industry with a view to creating new export models of weapons and modernizing existing arms and military equipment. It coordinated marketing, bids on contracts, and advertising operations, including the participation of Russian agents of MTC with foreign countries in international defense exhibitions. Analyzing various concepts, it was to take practical measures to establish finance-and-industry groups in Russia's defense complex, generate recommendations concerning participation of special export-import companies in such groups, and control the pricing of basic defense imports and exports. The Committee also coordinated reliability checks of foreign partners and provided audits of the foreign economic activity of Russian agents of military-technical cooperation.

In order to fulfill its mandate, the Committee on Military-Technical Cooperation was empowered to: suspend licenses if the participants of foreign economic activity violate established MTC procedures; receive foreign delegations occupied with similar problems as those faced by the Committee; send delegations abroad to facilitate military-technical cooperation; and participate in talks between the subjects of MTC and their foreign partners. The Committee was also authorized to supervise and effectively manage budget allocations for MTC programs; implementation of armament programs; limitation, disposal, and elimination of arms and munitions; and the conversion or contraction of the defense-industrial complex. The Committee was further authorized to issue acts within its competence with which all Russian subjects of MTC should comply, to control the execution of these acts, and to send its representatives to the Russian missions abroad upon agreement with the Ministry of Foreign Affairs and the Ministry of Foreign Economic Relations.

The Outlook for Enhancing the System of Export Controls

Only subsequent developments could reveal the effectiveness of the State Committee on Military-Technical Policy. Unfortunately, the creation of this "super-agency" repeated a past mistake—that is, blending the functions of both promoting and controlling arms sales to foreign markets. The Interdepartmental Commission for Military-Technical Cooperation of the Russia Federation with Foreign States eventually was subsumed under the Committee, which could objectively lead to the weakening of political control over arms trade exerted by foreign policy departments, the Ministry of Foreign Affairs and the External Intelligence Service.

One way out of this confusing situation could have been to leave the role of arms promotion to Rosvooruzheniye and the control functions to the State Committee. Another sensible measure could have been to remove the Commission for Military-Technical Cooperation from the framework of the State Committee and restore its "governmental" (i.e., super-departmental) status. As part of the reorganization of the Russian government, however, the State Committee on Military-Technical Policy was abolished in August 1996. In any case, the creation of the State Committee was a major step toward securing a strict state control in the field of arms trade and military-technical cooperation and therefore toward improving arms export control on the part of the executive. This remains the dominant trend in the evolution of a national system of export controls, and there is reason to believe that this trend will intensify in the future. Under Gen. Alexander Lebed, the Russian Security Council has attempted to win control over arms exports. The process of shaping a system and harmonizing it with the principles of international regimes has certainly been a learning experience for Russia!

The increasing sophistication of arms and military equipment has raised questions concerning the benefit of combining control mechanisms for both MTC and transfers of dual-use items and technologies. Today both mechanisms exist separately, on a bureaucratic level as well. One interdepartmental commission handles military-technical cooperation and another handles export controls. In highly developed nations, these mechanisms overlap. An international counter-proliferation regime would operate similarly. For example, the post-COCOM mechanism, the Wassenaar Arrangement, has been charged not only with control over conventional arms sales but also with non-proliferation of dual-use items.

In a much broader sense, Russia has not yet resolved a fundamental question: namely, the interrelation between arms export policy and national security policy. Two instruments of control over the spread of information vital for national security (one relating to state secrets, the other to control over the export of products and services that can be used to create various arms and military equipment) operate separately and irrespective of each other. At the same time, a clear-cut linkage among several export control regimes is lacking. One exists for the export of goods and services for military use, another for dual-use goods and services, and yet another for equipment, materials, and technologies used to develop missiles. This should be rectified. The process of classifying and declassifying data in the sphere of defense, economy, science and technology, and that of exporting, transfering, or exchanging data in such fields, should be complementary and regulated within a single framework.

Despite recent advances, Russia's system of export controls does not yet address four very particular spheres of state regulation:

- Control over the transfer of technologies, scientific and technical data in priority areas critical for sustaining the nation's military security.
- Control over state intellectual property and protection of property interests, including investment as a share of joint ventures in Russia and abroad, patenting abroad, the sale of licenses and know-how.
- Certification of international scientific and technical exchanges, in which the results of such activities are shared.
- Selective checks and inspections (including police inspections) of international scientific and technical exchanges in order to detect and prosecute transgressors of existing legislation.

In addition to these four functions, Russia's national control mechanism should perform the following roles:

- Balance and coordinate two parallel processes: cuts in state orders for procurement of arms and military equipment on the one hand, and conversion and diversification of military production on the other.
- Create and provide for the smooth operation of the market mechanisms to convert and diversify military industry and to dispose of arms and military equipment.
- Elaborate regulatory acts concerning inventory, stipulation and specification of property rights, and the use and disposal of earlier obtained results of scientific and technical activity.
- Model the enforcement mechanisms for intellectual property legislation and also create an information framework to facilitate conversion, turnover into joint-stock companies, and privatization of state enterprises.
- Ensure the application of the results of scientific and technical activity achieved while working on state contracts.
- Manage, regulate, and carry out international cooperation in military and dual-use technologies.

41

Realizing these proposals and carrying out the tasks delineated in the Statute of the State Committee of the Russian Federation on Military-Technical Policy should enable Russia to tackle the problems that need to be addressed effectively and comprehensively—and to engage the military-industrial complex in the process. It should also help maintain R&D and industrial capacity at satisfactory levels and secure state control not only over MTC programs but over this essential sector of Russian society.

Notes

[1]On June 25, 1996, President Yeltsin signed a decree formally endorsing what may be regarded as the first comprehensive national security concept. For its draft text, see *Politika natsionalnoy bezopasnosti Rossiyskoy Federatsii (1996-2000) Proekt.* Rossiyskiy Nauchnyy Fond, Federatsiya Mirai Soglasiya. Moscow, 1996, 49.

Chapter 4
Arms Export Controls: What Role for Parliament?

Yevgeni M. Kozhokin

The Role of Arms Exports in State Policy

Arms exports and other forms of military-technical cooperation are an essential part of a state's foreign and security policies, regardless of its political regime, social and economic order, or the nature of the relationship between its government, parliament, and military-industrial complex.

United States legislation describes arms exports as "a key instrument of U.S. national security and foreign policy" and as a major factor "providing for development of the military-industrial base and of the American economy as a whole."[1] Most American politicians and experts in the field of international security would support this view. According to Geoffrey Kemp, "arms sales played a major role in securing a victory in three critical wars of this century: World War I, World War II, and the Cold War."[2] U.S. arms also have provided for Israel's military superiority over its rivals, rendering an Arab military success in any conflict with Israel unlikely. The futility of military confrontation was one reason behind the PLO's attitude shift toward the Middle East peace process. Massive U.S. military assistance of all kinds during the 1970s and 1980s enabled Saudi Arabia to create advanced logistics systems, which in 1991 aided in the victory of the American-led coalition in the Persian Gulf War.

In 1986, the United States secretly endorsed the resumption of supplies of American arms by Israel to Iran, a country subject to U.S. embargo for supporting international terrorism. The decision to engage in secret U.S. arms transfers to Teheran was to serve the goals of "establishing a more moderate government in Iran, getting crucial intelligence information which could not be obtained otherwise regarding the intentions of the current government concerning its neighbors and terrorist acts, and the liberation of American hostages in Beirut." To further these goals, the U.S. government declared its intention to "support the attempt of third parties and third states to establish contacts with moderate elements inside and outside the Iranian government by supplying these elements with arms, equipment and other materials. This can enhance the credibility of their efforts to establish a more pro-American government in Iran by demonstrating their ability to secure resources needed to protect the country from Iraq and from the aggression of the Soviet Union."[3] The Clinton administration's policy to permit sales of fighters, tanks, and other offensive weapons to ten countries in the former Eastern Bloc not only provides new potential clients for the U.S. military industry but also brings former Soviet satellites into the U.S. sphere of influence.

While France takes an essentially similar approach to the arms trade, it places greater emphasis on the theory and practice of its financial aspects. In its 1994 Defense White Paper, the French government overtly claims that "being the main source of self-financing for national industry and guaranteeing the necessary level of industrial and technical proficiency, arms exports have enabled us to match the demands of our policy of autonomy in the field of arms production with constraints inherent in the size of our country and our armed forces and in the share of the budgetary means that the country can allot for its military equipment. Moreover, arms export is one instrument of our foreign policy that contributes to France's presence on the global scene."[4] Cognizant of budgetary limits, the French leadership relies principally on currency proceeds from arms sales to support the defense industry and maintain France's national defense requirements.

China's arms export policy is unique. Augmenting arms exports is part of China's strategy to obtain resources for the technological modernization of its military industry. In order to raise the technological sophistication of its exports, China has undertaken joint projects with Russia, Israel, and the West. Foreign investment plays a central role in modernizing China's military industry and enhancing its competitiveness. By 1993 foreign investment bolstered 158 major military enterprises, some of which became joint-stock companies with stocks traded overseas.[5] Since the second half of the 1980s, technological progress in Chinese arms production has accelerated so much that China is gradually catching up with its main competitors. Zhuhai-class torpedo-boat destroyers of 4,500 tons displacement, for example, are equipped with an American LM 2500 turbogas engine, Italian A244S torpedoes, a French C^3 system, and French Crotale anti-aircraft missiles. Chinese ship-building technology was instantly upgraded from 1950s levels to the Western level of the 1970s.

Thanks to modern technology transfers, new Chinese tank guns, military radar, missiles, and computers now compete on the international weapons market. Apparently many foreign buyers are more content than the People's Liberation Army (PLA) itself to purchase certain Chinese weapons systems. The established scheme proceeds first with the introduction of advanced technology, then with the refinement of tactical and technical specifications of the weapons system, followed by testing of the system by a foreign army. Currently China buys more arms than its sells, but if it ventures into new export fields and develops high-tech weapon models, it may ultimately become a serious competitor in the shrinking international arms market.

Russia's arms export policy is similar to that of other leading suppliers. However, while military-technical cooperation of the Russian Federation with foreign countries should address Russia's national security interests, the relevant draft legislation says nothing about arms export as an instrument of foreign policy. This so-called "American approach" does not appeal widely to civil servants responsible for this sector of foreign trade. Quite the opposite: Attempts are sometimes made to subject Russian foreign policy to export needs. At the same time, the view that foreign policy is above economic interests remains strong. Russia has a long way to go before it can sensibly balance its economic interests, foreign policy needs, and legal and moral imperatives. Russia is also grappling with certain policy extremes, such as a super-ideological foreign policy and opportunistic pragmatism.[6]

Arms transfers are executed by state companies; by private companies under the control of the state or subsidized by the state; or by private companies and individuals outside state control (the black market). State policy should attempt to control arms exports from infringing on other state interests on the international scene. As a rule, controls are overseen by executive bodies in the exporting state. However, confining the system of control only to governmental bureaucracy may be unwise. The opportunities for corruption and abuses of authority are markedly lower if an arms export control system involves national parliaments. The experience of other countries in this respect is of considerable interest to the Russian Federation, which has just started to construct a legal democratic state.

Western Experiences with Parliamentary Arms Export Control

United States

When assessing the American experience, one must bear in mind that the U.S. Congress is a special body of authority. Unlike those in Europe, U.S. parliamentary committees play a strong role in arms export control. Committees have long been "a central structural element of Congress, and their history in many respects reflects the history of the nation and of the Congress."[7]

Congress acquired arms export control functions in the mid-1970s, during a period when the overall political influence of the legislature was on the rise. The Budget Supervision and Funds Freezing Act adopted in 1974 significantly reinforced the analytical base of legislative decision-making on budgetary issues and enabled the making of a separate legislative budget. This reform secured the centralization of the budgetary process within the legislative branch and the establishment of a division for National Security and International Relations within the Congressional Budget Office. This division was authorized to evaluate the Pentagon's budget as well as foreign military and economic aid programs.

U.S. legislation makes a clear distinction between conventional arms exports and the transfer of technologies that could

46

enable the production of weapons of mass destruction. Legislation on conventional weapons empowers Congress to ban a specific deal. Legislation on the export of technologies is elaborated in greater detail. The Arms Export Control Act (1976) encourages intra-governmental military-technical cooperation over direct conventional arms sales between private companies and foreign governments, which serves to increase the authority of Congress in arms transfer decision-making.

According to the 1976 Act, the President must furnish Congress advance written notification of any arms transfers over $14 million. The Act also stipulates the conditions under which the President may consent to third country re-transfers of American equipment. One such condition is the written obligation of the third country not to resell these arms without the approval of the U.S. government. In August 1986, another provision was added to the Arms Export Control Act, prohibiting U.S. arms sales to countries supporting international terrorism.

Western Europe

In Western Europe, the power of parliament is generally more restricted. This is certainly the case with control over the national arms trade. Neither the British Parliament, the French National Assembly, nor the German Bundestag have committees that could exert such control.

The British Parliament has no special oversight role, but it can be kept informed through ministerial statements to the House of Commons and the sending of official pages to the Library of the House. When arms transfer policy becomes contentious, however, as was retroactively the case with sales to Iraq in the 1980s, debate in the Commons can heat up. Prime Minister John Major was forced to set up a special inquiry, headed by Sir Richard Scott, a high-ranking judge. His 2,000-page report severely criticized the lack of legislative involvement in the setting of policy.

When, in the wake of the Persian Gulf War, France was criticized for its 1980s arms sales to Iraq, proposals were made to increase the role of the National Assembly in decisions on arms sales. In response, the French Ministry of Defense advised the Defense Affairs Commission of the National Assembly about major arms contracts. However, this procedure has not been regularized, and parliament has become quiet on the issue.

Permanent commissions of the French National Assembly exert only limited control of arms exports, and that is over financial aspects. Ministers may attend commission meetings if they so request. They can also be summoned to the Commission by its chairman, acting through the Speaker of the Chamber and the Prime Minister.

The German legislature has control functions, but implementation is largely restricted by considerations of political expediency. The ruling coalition, which controls all committees of the Bundestag and seeks to strengthen the party's position in Government, is not interested in burdening the Bundestag with a "discomforting" level of control. Procedurally, the possibilities for an effective control system in the sphere of arms exports are limited. The Bundestag could call for an investigative commission, which would convene a working group of independent experts to provide the legislature with concrete recommendations.

Parliamentary hearings attended by experts and lobbyists can also facilitate control. The Bundestag presents minor and major interpellations to the Government in order to obtain information. Minor interpellations usually receive written responses. Major inquiries often provoke a broad oral discussion. Further means of control include the "Question Hour," when representatives of the Government answer inquiries from the deputies. During the weekly Question Hours, deputies may direct two oral inquiries to Government representatives. If an immediate answer is deferred, inquirers receive one later in writing. The Question Hour is closely linked with the "Actual Hour," a one-hour exchange of opinions on a focused topic. Actual Hours are generally organized when deputies are left unsatisfied with the explanations of government representatives during a Question Hour, but they occasionally occur irrespective of previous inquiries. A new supervisory instrument is the formal questioning of the Government, which takes place immediately after the meeting of the Cabinet of Ministers. For half an hour, deputies can pose topical questions regarding Cabinet meetings to relevant members of the Federal Government.

The most effective instruments of the deputies are probably committees for the investigation of abuse, commissioned on demand of one-fourth of the Bundestag. These serve to clear up suspicions of political and administrative abuse. For instance, the Defense Committee can decide to be transformed into a commission for the investigation of abuse. The Bundestag Commissioner on Defense also has control functions.

The full Bundestag only occasionally addresses questions of arms export control—generally in specific cases commanding public attention and media coverage. For example, after the Federal Security Council rejected a proposal to sell ten German submarines to Taiwan in 1993, a group of Bundestag deputies from the Budget, Defense, and Foreign Policy Committees attempted to appeal the Council's ruling. This "friends of Taipei" association rallied almost one-fifth of the deputies in the lower chamber.[8] In some instances, such as the suspension of arms sales to Turkey in 1994, discussion can even be taken to the level of the *Landtag* (regional parliaments).[9] *Landtag* sessions are characterized not only by lobbying against extensive German arms trade but also by the promotion of German arms sales.

Since 1982, special regulations endorsed by the Government of the Federal Republic of Germany have been effective in limiting the export of German arms to countries outside the NATO area and to unstable regions if "vital national interests" are not at stake. The *Lander* government of Lower Saxony even sought to have a provision included in the Constitution that would ban such exports.

After it was disclosed that German companies had supplied missile technology components to Saddam Hussein's regime in Iraq, public outcry and embarrassment led the Bundestag to increase the penalty for illegal trade in advanced military equipment. Company directors who deliberately contribute to the unauthorized proliferation of military technology can be sentenced to a minimum of two years in prison. German arms sales to Turkey, a NATO member, became highly controversial after 1992. The publication of photographs showing tanks of the former German Democratic Republic (GDR) being used by the Turkish army in their counter-insurgency against the Kurdish P.K.K. movement compelled the temporary suspension of further arms sales. Yet arms sales resumed just three months later, after Ankara gave Bonn a written pledge to use German weapons for legitimate external defense needs only.

Despite such limitations, Germany successfully competes with traditional major arms suppliers on the world market. German military industry leaders have complained that the restrictions are too tight, and they have rather successfully attempted to ease them. For example, South Korea may be accorded the same status as a NATO country, so that it can freely buy German military equipment. Prior to the conclusion of the Wassenaar Arrangement, some proposed revising the export restrictions on dual-use items to focus on only two areas, weapons of mass destruction and missile technology, thereby abolishing restrictions on exports of dual-use conventional items altogether.

The Russian Parliament's Recent Experience with Arms Export Control

As Russia attempted to establish a modern Parliament, it had to overcome the Soviet tradition of combining all legislative, executive, and administrative powers in one supreme body of state authority. Before September 1993, the Congress of People's Deputies filled this role. The standing body of the Congress was the Supreme Soviet. According to Article 117 of the Constitution, all state and public agencies, organizations, and officials were obliged to comply with requests of commissions of the chambers and commissions and committees of the Supreme Soviet of the Russian Federation, and to submit to them all requisite materials and documentation. Therefore, according to the letter of the law, until September 1993, the Russian Parliament had the possibility to exert complete control over arms exports. The Committee for Defense and Security has repeatedly emphasized the need for a mechanism of parliamentary control in this field. However, controls were not secured by either the 1990-93 Supreme Soviet or the first Duma in 1993-95.

In 1992, a working group on military-technical cooperation (MTC) was set up within the Committee for Industry and Power Economy, headed by Deputy Chairman V. Ya. Vitebsky. The working group was composed of representatives of the committees for International Affairs; Foreign Trade; Industry and Energy; Defense and Security; and Budget, Planning, Taxes, and Prices. Endorsed by the Presidium of the Supreme Soviet, the group was charged with the supervision of arms exports and the drafting of resolutions for the Presidium of the Supreme Soviet concerning annual plans for MTC, as well as individual deals not yet included. This involved large transactions (those exceeding $15 million), supplies transacted on credit or grant military aid, and also supplies of certain kinds of arms to be stipulated later. According to Vitebsky, the group considered itself to be an arm of the Presidium, although, unlike the latter, it did not have veto rights. The deputies had good working contacts with the Ministry of Foreign Economic Relations, the Commission for Military-Technical Cooperation, and other agencies dealing with MTC, so that potential problems could be solved at an early stage without too much conflict.[10] Meetings were held to discuss the concept of the law on military-technical cooperation prepared by the Ministry of Foreign Economic Relations. The working group defined three types of MTC contracts: large contracts requiring consideration by the Presidium of the Supreme Soviet; contracts to be drawn up with the participation of members of the parliamentary group; and other contracts.

In spring 1993, L. B. Gurevich submitted a memorandum on the need to create an Expert Council on MTC to the Chief of Presidential Administration Sergei Filatov and to First Deputy Prime Minister Vladimir Shumeiko, then head of the Commission for Military-Technical Cooperation. However, this memo received little attention at that point. The Security Council of the Russian Federation also participated in the preparation of the draft law on military-technical cooperation. The work was coordinated by Secretary of the Security Council Yuri Skokov and involved one or two members of the Committee for Defense and Security of the Supreme Soviet. It is difficult to assess how much has been implemented of what was decided in 1992-93.

Since the termination of the Supreme Soviet's activities in October 1993, an authoritarian approach to parliamentarianism has prevailed in Russia. While the new Constitution adopted on December 12, 1993, defines the Federal Assembly (Russia's two-chamber Parliament) as a representative and legislative body, the body lacks control and administrative functions. The Constitution does not provide for the rights of the committees in both chambers: the Council of the Federation,

51

the upper house, and the State Duma, the lower house. A deputy can make inquiries to a ministry or executive agency; however, neither the Federal Assembly, nor the chamber, the committee, or the deputy has strong leverage power to obtain exhaustive information.

On February 9, 1994, after examining the Draft Law on Foreign Economic Activity submitted by the Government, the Duma sent it to committees for consideration. Committees were to submit amendments to the Committee for Economic Policy by February 23. Article 17 of the Draft Law deals entirely with export controls. Its provisions generally look like framework conditions, partly because of the uncertain future of some agencies and partly because of inter-agency rivalry. For instance, the article stipulates that "the nomenclature of specific kinds of raw materials, substances, equipment, technologies, scientific and technical information and services that can be used for the creation of weapons of mass destruction and missile delivery vehicles, as well as the most dangerous kinds of weapons subject to export control, is defined in the registers endorsed by the President upon proposal of the Government." These lists should be made public and the procedure of control determined by the Government.

The Duma also considered the law on military-technical cooperation. As early as 1991, Gennadi Burbulis, State Secretary of the Russian Federation, tried to set up a working group for drafting the law on MTC. At that time, the effort was lost. Only in 1994 was the draft document generated by experts at the Ministry of Foreign Economic Relations forwarded to the Committee on Defense.

This bill assumed that foreign military-technical cooperation is exclusively state-controlled through the current system of permits. Third country re-export of Russian arms and military equipment is permitted only with the authorization of the Russian Government. According to the Draft Law, the Federal Assembly is empowered to consider and adopt legislation in the field of military-technical cooperation and to examine presidential decisions on foreign military aid. The Draft Law corresponded to the relatively weak political profile of the Federal Assembly in 1993-95, when the Parliament, elected for only two years, had little chance to improve its standing.

The current Federal Assembly, especially the second Duma, might face a different reality. Four-year terms are likely to produce a constructive state of mind among deputies. A clear-cut constitutional environment will also compel Parliament to look for unorthodox ways to enhance its role. With a longer mandate, deputies elected in 1995 will acquire a corporate mentality. Despite their political affiliations, they will seek to protect some democratic principles for the simple reason that if they are not observed, Parliament may not survive as an institution.

Parliament's growing role gives it leverage in areas where it lacked it before. While strong parliamentary control over the arms trade is a matter for the future, Russia must start moving toward this goal today.

Russian Arms Trade Legislation

In Russia, the regulatory base for MTC includes presidential decrees and various provisions and rulings issued by the Government. Since the bureaucratic chaos of 1991, this regulatory base has been constantly expanding and changing. Between late 1991 and August 1992, when a licensing system for the export of military production was introduced, an intricate system of export permits evolved, including individual permits issued to producers by the Government or upon the instruction of the President. Permits were issued for distinct deals as well as for specific terms (e.g., one month, half a year). The system of permits involved only executive bodies; Parliament was barred from any arms export control functions.

An Interdepartmental Commission for Military-Technical Cooperation of the Russian Federation with Foreign States was set up in March 1992 to control arms exports. In the same month, the Law on Conversion of Military Industry in the Russian Federation was adopted. A special section of this Law regulated foreign economic activities of enterprises undergoing conversion. The Law entitled such enterprises to export raw matter, materials, and equipment discharged in the course of conversion, with some exceptions. First of all, enterprises in the process of conversion were required to carry out foreign economic activity in compliance with existing legislation. Second, export of almost all dual-use technologies (items that could be used for producing civilian goods) was subject to a ban. Third, Article 10 reinforced the state's central regulatory role in all aspects of MTC in order to protect and advance Russia's military, political, and economic interests.[11]

In April 1992, President Yeltsin signed a Decree on the Measures to Create Export Controls in the Russian Federation. A Commission for Export Controls was established in compliance with the Decree, comprising deputy heads of the following ministries and departments: Ministry of Foreign Affairs, Ministry of Economy, Ministry of Defense, Ministry of Science, Higher Education and Technical Policy, Ministry of Industry, Ministry of Foreign Economic Relations, State Customs Committee of the Russian Federation, Ministry of Security, Committee for the Protection of Economic Interests of the Russian Federation under the President, State Committee for the Supervision Over Nuclear and Radiation Security under the President of the Russian Federation, and the Russian Academy of Sciences.

In May 1992, the Presidential Decree on Military-Technical Cooperation of the Russian Federation with Foreign Countries was signed. It vested functions of coordination and control in the Interdepartmental Commission for Military-Technical Cooperation. This agency was charged with coordinating bilateral and multilateral intergovernmental commissions on MTC, licensing third-country sales of arms and military equipment manufactured by foreign states with Russian assistance, and endorsing documents concerning procedures for MTC. Essential control functions were also vested in the Ministry of Foreign Affairs, which supervises Russia's compliance with international obligations and assures that all participants in MTC respect the political interests of the Russian Federation.[12] No mention of Parliament is found in this Decree.

Licenses for military exports issued by the Ministry of Foreign Economic Relations were introduced in August 1992. Almost all arms export decisions were then in the hands of specialized state agencies: the Main Department for Collaboration and Cooperation of the Ministry of Foreign Economic Relations, Oboronexport, Spetsvneshtechnika, Voyentech, Promexport, and a number of others. The existence of several state agencies engaged in arms export, especially when their competencies were not clearly defined, allowed for abuse, and complicated the process of control. In November 1993, Rosvooruzheniye, a single specialized State Company for arms export and import was created, and it gained the right to issue licenses for MTC. Arms export finally became centralized.

Defense enterprises lobbied in 1993 for the right to export independently. As a result, the Statute on Certification and Registration of the Right of Enterprises to Export Arms, Military Equipment, and Works and Services for Military Needs was endorsed one year later. Certified defense enterprises were now entitled to seek foreign clients in the countries with which MTC was not prohibited, to exhibit arms and military equipment receiving export clearance, to disclose their tactical and technical specifications during talks, to quote an approximate price, and to carry out marketing. Most important, they could independently sign contracts and export arms, military equipment, and works and services in excess of state defense orders according to the specifications of their licenses.

After the Statute had been adopted, it seemed that the defense industry's position on a number of issues, advanced through the State Committee for Defense Industries, was being reinforced. The agencies assessing the political consequences of any arms deals were only involved in decision-making at final stages. Parliament is indirectly mentioned in the Statute one time—regarding the procedure for suspending the operations of defense enterprises. However, while the Statute reflected a new bureaucratic balance among the various bodies involved in MTC, in reality it has never been implemented.

In December 1994, President Yeltsin signed a decree on the creation of the State Committee of the Russian Federation on Military-Technical Policy. On paper, the new agency had a broad range of basic responsibilities, including elaboration of draft laws in the field of MTC and military-industrial policy, implementation of actual state policy, coordination of activities of the various federal bodies in weapons production, conversion of defense industry, arms reduction and utilization, and the exercise of export control.

The principal function vested in the State Committee was licensing and the suspension of licenses. With an eye on paying off Russia's foreign debt with arms exports, the State Committee participated in talks on the settlement of external debts. The State Committee was also supposed to solve the delicate problem of verifying the exact terms of arms transfers, including components and spare parts, bearing in mind Russian compliance with various multilateral treaties on military-technical cooperation.

In implementing the control functions conferred by the Statute, the State Committee would have enjoyed considerable powers. It was entitled to obtain information from ministries and departments, specialized companies, and defense enterprises, and planned to set up an information network. It was also authorized to send representatives to foreign missions upon the agreement of the Ministry of Foreign Affairs and the Ministry of Foreign Economic Relations. If fully implemented, the State Committee of the Russian Federation on the Military-Technical Policy would have managed a highly centralized system of arms export control. Regulatory control and direct management of Russian companies engaged in MTC would have been concentrated in a single agency. However, in August 1996, before it had a chance to fully develop all of these functions, the Committee was abolished, and its functions were transferred to the Russian Security Council.

Notes

[1]National Defense Authorization Act for FY 1994. Washington: U.S. GPO, 1993, 183.

[2]Geoffrey Kemp. "The Continuing Debate over U.S. Arms Sales: Strategic Needs and the Quest for Arms Limitations." *The Annals of the American Academy of Political and Social Sciences*, September 1994, 147.

[3]V. A. Nikonov. *Afera Iran-Contras*. Moscow, 1987, 23.

[4]France, White Paper on National Defense 1994, 124.

[5]*Guide to International Assistance and Investment in Conversion of China's Military Industry*. Chinese Society for the Peaceful Use of Military Industry, 1993.

[6]See, for instance, the statements of Mikhail Malei, proposing a massive launch of not only arms but also nuclear materials on the foreign market (*Izvestiya*, March 31, 1992). Such statements obviously have a negative impact. Unfortunately, they are sometimes interpreted abroad regardless of the actual state of affairs in Russian politics, or common practices in Russian arms exports. Cf. Richard F. Staar, *The New Russian Armed Forces. Preparing for War or Peace?* Hoover Institution, Stanford University Press, 1994, 10.

[7]Steven S. Smith and Christopher J. Deering. *Committees in Congress*. Washington, 1990, 1.

[8]*Der Spiegel*, February 22, 1993, 30-31.

[9]*Der Spiegel*, April 11, 1994.

[10]On the plans of the group, see Vitebsky's interview to *Nezavisimaya Gazeta*, July 11, 1992.

[11]*Sbornik zakonodatel'nykh aktov Rossiyskoy Federatsii* (Collection of Legislative Acts of the Russian Federation), Volume XI, Moscow, 1992, 84.

[12]*Sbornik ukazov Presidenta RF* (Collection of Decrees of the President of the Russian Federation), No. 322-1474, April-November 1992, 59-60.

Chapter 5

Russia, the Arms Trade, and Military-Political Stability in the Middle East

Vitaly V. Naumkin

A Middle East Arms Race

The Middle East, a region composed of some of the most militarized nations in the world, is one of the largest markets for arms and military equipment. Since the end of World War II, the region has been an arena in which many protracted and bloody armed conflicts have been played out. For almost a decade, Middle East nations have been acquiring numerous, sophisticated military technologies. Notwithstanding these realities, a defusion of tensions and the accords in recent years between Israel and its Arab neighbors bring hope for enhanced stability and security in the region.

Conventional arms proliferation in the Middle East is an issue that must be analyzed in its proper context, taking into account several considerations:

1. Conventional arms proliferation must be assessed in conjunction with the proliferation of nuclear arms and other weapons of mass destruction. Israel's undeclared possession of nuclear weapons, the "near threshold" nuclear status of other nations, and recent uses of chemical weapons are all factors that have fueled a regional arms race.

2. Arms races in the Middle East are prompted not only by deep-seated animosities incited by long and fierce wars between countries in the (e.g., Arab states vs. Israel, Iran vs. Iraq, Iraq vs. Kuwait) but also by outstanding conflicts that may provoke future conflicts, such as the fate of the

Kurds, an equitable division of water resources, and territorial disputes.

3. Apart from external threats, internal security problems are characteristic of the region; separatism and other armed political, ethnic, and religious opposition movements are rife.

4. Some nations have become fully or partially self-sufficient in weapons production and now export many types of armaments.

5. The Middle East has become an area of intense competition among the major arms exporting countries, each of which has its own set of economic incentives to sell defense equipment abroad. Vast financial resources from energy deposits have enabled most states to purchase their huge military arsenals.

6. The quantity of weapons accumulated by some nations largely exceeds their legitimate defense requirements.

Arms stockpiling creates chain reactions: Excessive arms purchases encourage competing states to acquire weapons of equal or greater quality in a perfect illustration of the security dilemma. No doubt deterring potential threats compels Middle Eastern nations to maintain high defense capabilities. Within reasonable limits, arms supplies can enhance regional military and political stability. However, gross disparities in real military power, economic development, geographic size, and population make it impossible for some states to guarantee their security with their own resources. They must rely on external security guarantees, erect regional/collective security structures, or seek other modes of self-protection.

Since the end of the Cold War, arms transfers have been negotiated almost exclusively as sales, rather than the grant military aid more typical of the past. As is the case with the global arms trade, the United States retains the largest market share of sales to the Middle East. From 1992 to 1995, the market share was divided among the major exporters as follows: United States (56 percent), Western Europe (34 percent), and Russia (5 percent).[1]

North Korea and the People's Republic of China have aggressively pushed to gain a foothold in the Middle East arms market. Facing steep competition, Russia has been striving to retain and expand its own position, resuming arms deliveries to Iran, Cyprus, Turkey, and Syria, and advocating a relaxation of U.N. sanctions against Iraq. Russian arms manufacturers actively participated in arms exhibitions in the United Arab Emirates with an eye toward entering the arms market of the Persian Gulf Cooperation Council (GCC).

For instance, at the IDEX-95 arms exhibition in the Emirates, Russian arms exporters promoted T-80 tanks, Msta-S artillery systems with Krasnopol guided munitions, Tunguska artillery and missile systems, Tor, Buk and S-300 air defense systems, Metis and Konkurs anti-tank missile systems, and many other products.[2]

Various factors have led to the military balance and equipment composition pattern shown in Table 2. The remaining weapons are imported primarily from France, Britain, and the

Table 2
Importers and Sources of Imports in the Persian Gulf Region (percentages)

Importing Nations	Major Sources of Imports of Armored Vehicles	Major Sources of Imports of Aircraft and Missiles
Bahrain	USA: 100%	USA: 100%
Iran	Russia: 80%	Russia: 50%; USA: 50%
Iraq	Russia: 90%	Russia: 90%
Jordan	USA: 90%	USA: 70%
Qatar	USA: 90%	France: 80%
Kuwait	USA: 90%	Britain: 60%
United Arab Emirates	USA: 80%	France: 90%
Oman	USA: 50%	France: 80%
Saudi Arabia	USA: 90%	USA:
Syria	Russia: 100%	Russia.

Source: Zarubezhnoye Voyennoye Obozreniye, 1995, no.3.

61

Table 3
Leading Importers of Conventional Arms in the Middle East, 1992-1995 (deliveries in millions of 1995 US dollars)

Importing Nations	Deliveries
Saudi Arabia	$30,000
Egypt	5,700
Kuwait	3,100
Israel	2,700
Iran	2,600
United Arab Emirates	1,800
Oman	800
Syria	700
Iraq	0

Source: Congressional Research Service, Conventional Arms Transfers to Developing Nations (1988-1995).

People's Republic of China. The value of conventional arms imports per country is shown in Table 3.

Arms export rivalry parallels and has been stimulated by a struggle between regional centers of power for domination of the Middle East. According to analysts at the Institute of Oriental Studies of the Russian Academy of Sciences, between 1985 and 1990, annual expenses on arms imports in the Middle East rose from $8.2 billion to $18.8 billion (or by 2.3 times). In 1995, defense imports constituted roughly $21 billion for the region. Western experts predict further growth in the Middle East arms market—to top $55 billion by 2000. Of this amount, $15 billion is expected to be spent on naval modernization, $30 billion on air force modernization, and about $10 billion on miscellaneous armaments including tanks.[3]

The market for arms and military technology is unique for each country in the Middle East. Arms imports are more prevalent in those nations in which arms manufacturing is lacking or insufficient. This is true of the Arabian peninsula; however, the establishment of a modern military-industrial complex and foreign military-technical cooperation based on offsets is well under way there. Offsets require arms-supplying nations to invest a certain percentage of any deals in the domestic economic development of the importing country. Offsets frequently involve the development of military infrastructure. This strategy is most actively pursued by the United Arab Emirates.

Arms Deliveries and Regional Military-Political Stability

Large military stockpiles in the Middle East have helped to maintain regional military and political stability. Yet while extensive arsenals have provided regimes with the capability to repulse threats, they have repeatedly failed to prevent conflicts from breaking out—to the great detriment of the population and the environment. Enormous defense spending has also heavily burdened national economies.

The end of the Cold War produced hope that the nations of the Middle East would no longer be clients of global alliances and that regional confrontations would vanish. Instead, the accumulation of huge amounts of conventional weaponry facilitated new types of conflicts, such as Iraq's invasion of Kuwait. Even though Iraq relied on massive arms imports, Kuwait and its Gulf allies failed to resist the invasion despite all of their modern weapons. This was regarded by some as another proof that invasions can be stopped only by an external power.

With the consent of the Gulf states—in particular, Saudi Arabia—an American rapid reaction force was deployed and was considered a major instrument to protect the security of these countries. On the other hand, when Iraqi missile attacks targeted Israel, the Israeli government decided that foreign aid could not arrive in time to defend against a large-scale offensive. Israel continues to strengthen its own deterrence capabilities and to maintain regional military superiority. This likely includes nuclear weapons as a deterrent of last resort. Apparently having huge conventional arsenals led Iraq to believe that it could achieve political goals through military means. Desert Storm demonstrated the decisive role of military policy factors in the development of regional situations.

A Western commitment to free navigation of the Persian Gulf and to uninterrupted oil supplies would enhance the general stability of the region. The industrialized world will continue to depend on the energy resources of the Middle East and, therefore, will seek to maintain regional stability and help repulse internal and external threats to moderate Arab regimes.

Desert Storm did not stop regional sabre-rattling, however. Recent incidents provoked by Iraq include a civil war in Yemen and a Turkish expedition into Iraqi Kurdistan. Despite the small scale of these incidents, they display potential for future conflicts. Moderate states in the Gulf are not insured against domestic upheavals; military capabilities do not guarantee regime survival. Saudi Arabia, for example, cannot exclude the emergence of a fundamentalist or a populist movement opposed to the ruling family.

The most serious regional dispute, the Arab-Israeli conflict, is gradually coming to a settlement. Yet the Middle East is still far from becoming a safe haven. Many regional leaders still view a high level of military preparedness as essential to their national security.

Iran's Rearmament Efforts

Iran's growth in military strength and defense industrial capabilities stems from a long-term rearmament program adopted in the early 1990s for the armed forces and the Islamic Revolutionary Guards. Believed to cost roughly $25 billion (a little over half of that amount was spent by 1991),[4] the program includes replacing U.S. combat aircraft purchased in the 1970s with modern Russian warplanes, acquiring sophisticated Russian and Chinese arms and technologies, and expanding Iran's submarine fleet. Special attention has been placed on modernizing existing surface-to-surface missile technology and purchasing North Korean Nodon-1 two-stage missiles, which are capable of carrying both chemical and nuclear warheads.[5]

Germany, the People's Republic of China, and lately Russia have been active in the Iranian arms market. Germany has been Iran's traditional supplier of missiles. In the 1980s, Frantz

Werner Industrie-Ausruestung supplied the technology to build Arasch tactical missiles and helped launch their production at a military facility near Teheran (Parchin). Technical and economic assistance from Orbital Transport-und Raketen Geselschaft (OTRAG) allowed Iran to build a surface-to-air missile test site in the vicinity of Sultanabad. German experts also assisted the modernization program for a missile site in Semnan. In accordance with a ten-year scientific and technical cooperation agreement signed in 1990, China has also taken steps to help develop Iran's military industry.

Since the early 1990s, Western nations have expressed concern over the military aspects of expanded Russian-Iranian cooperation in the nuclear field. According to a 1993 agreement, Russia pledged to supply Iran two research and two industrial nuclear reactors. In January 1995, the agreement was extended with a special protocol. Press reports suggested that the protocol was related to the completion of Unit One ("Busher"), a nuclear power plant in southern Iran whose construction was suspended by Germany. Other measures included Russian assistance in extracting uranium deposits; delivery of a Russian 30-50 megawatt light hydrogen reactor, ostensibly "for research purposes"; construction of other reactors in Iran; and training for Iranian nuclear experts in Russia. The total cost of the projects amounts to $800 million.[6]

Nuclear cooperation deserves discussion, due to the specific circumstances. American suspicions about Iran's nuclear weapons program were first voiced in 1992 by CIA Director Robert Gates. But the International Atomic Energy Agency (IAEA) mission to Iran in 1992 failed to find evidence incompatible with the peaceful use of nuclear power and radiation at inspected sites (including Moallem-Kala) at the specific time of the inspection.[7] The report did little to assuage Western concern. In 1992, U.S. President George Bush remarked to Congress that, "Iran is in the early stages of developing its nuclear arms." Washington persuaded the group of advanced industrialized nations (the G-7 countries) to tighten sanctions on the delivery of nuclear materials to both Iran and Libya. In February 1993, CIA Director James Woolsey stated that Iran was attempting to acquire nuclear weapons, even though it is a party to the Nuclear Non-Proliferation Treaty.[8]

The U.S. administration has failed to secure a total embargo on nuclear cooperation; Russia, China, and a number of other countries continue to collaborate with Iran in this sphere. Similarly, the United States has failed to persuade European nations and international organizations to impose a trade embargo on Iran. The intention of such an embargo would be to retard the growth of Iran's military potential and perhaps force a change in its foreign policy, particularly toward a Middle East settlement.

Russian experts allege that the Russian-Iranian deal could not help Iran obtain nuclear weapons. They suspect that the West seeks to prevent Moscow from entering the high-technology market. At the same time, Russia is concerned about Iran's autonomous nuclear weapons production capabilities, as stated in a non-confidential report of the Russian Foreign Intelligence Service. Iran's nuclear ambitions have been openly disclosed in Teheran. As Iranian Vice President Ayatollah Mohajerani declared in October 1991, since Israel "possesses a nuclear device, Moslem countries should have the same potential."[9] Some Russian scientists, like leading ecologist and one-time presidential advisor Alexei Yablokov, believe that the nuclear power plant Russia wishes to build in Iran could lead to the development of Iranian nuclear weapons.[10] Iran is reported to have established a secret network of ten nuclear research centers for its nuclear program, including an underground base in Moallem-Kala and new uranium enrichment facilities in Keredge.[11]

According to V. E. Novikov, an expert at the Russian Institute of Strategic Studies, there are several nuclear sites in Iran: the Nuclear Research Centre (Teheran), the Nuclear Technology Centre (Isfahan), the Nuclear Research Centre for Agriculture and Medicine (Keredge), and a nuclear facility in Moallem-Kala (north of Teheran). No facility has the capability of producing weapons-grade nuclear fission materials at this time, and no illicit deliveries of nuclear raw materials or nuclear fuel to Iran have been reported.[12] The Russian Foreign Intelligence Service believes that, with extensive financing and determination, Iran could produce nuclear weapons as early as the year 2000.[13] The majority of Russian and foreign experts believe the development of an Iranian nuclear device will take at least a decade. However, the illicit acquisition of weapons-grade uranium or plutonium could accelerate this process.

Russian leaders held that the nuclear plant construction did not violate the principles of nuclear non-proliferation. They expressed Russia's intention to assist the world community in imposing tough international control over implementation of non-proliferation and to continue to discuss the matter in the framework of the commission set up by U.S. Vice President Albert Gore and Russian Premier Viktor Chernomyrdin. President Yeltsin admitted in the spring of 1995 that the contract with Iran had initially included military and civilian aspects, and that the former were re-examined to exclude production of weapons-grade fuel.

Nuclear contracts between Russia and Iran will continue to pose problems for Russian-American relations—especially given negative public and congressional opinion in the United States. Attempts to link U.S.-Russian relations to the fate of the Russian-Iranian contract (e.g., by threatening to cancel all U.S. aid if the contract is not abandoned) jeopardize the present state of bilateral relations.

Russian-Iranian Military-Technical Cooperation

An accurate assessment of Russian-Iranian military cooperation is limited by a paucity of exact data from official Russian and Iranian sources and the diverse and sometimes incompatible data provided by international and other national sources.

In the late 1970s, the U.S.S.R. approached Iran, then under the Shah, to sell armored vehicles and to commence military cooperation in the field of naval weaponry, but this initiative did not result in any sales. After the Islamic revolution of 1979, Soviet-Iranian military cooperation developed slowly. The main factors preventing the U.S.S.R. from forging stronger bilateral defense ties included Moscow's concern over the prospect of Iranian arms supplies to Afghan *mujaheddin*, then at war with the Soviet Union, and over Iraq's Friendship Treaty with Moscow at a time when Iraq was engaged in an ongoing war with Iran. After the Gulf War, the Soviet withdrawal from

Afghanistan, and Teheran's de facto repudiation of a policy to export Islamic revolution, Russian reservations to supply arms to Iran abated. Nevertheless, Iran was able to turn to other suppliers for modern weapons if its requests to Moscow were blocked.

Starting in 1990, the situation changed dramatically. Russia began supplying Iran with some models of armored vehicles (BTR-50p floating armored personnel carriers, BMP infantry fighting vehicles); BM-21 Grad multiple-launch rocket systems; ZSU-57-2 SPAAG and SU-23-4 "Shilka" (Quad) anti-aircraft systems; Strela-type (SA-9 Gaskin) shoulder-launched anti-aircraft missiles; ZU-23 anti-aircraft guns; small arms; and a large number of military vehicles including prime movers with trailers for towing military materiel.[14] According to American expert Zalmay Khalilzad: "Due to the Western embargo in the 1980s, Iran was forced to buy arms from Russia, China, Eastern Europe, and other Third World countries. Initially, China was the most important supplier. In the 1990s, however, Russia has become the largest and the most important supplier of conventional weapons to Iran."[15]

Khalilzad's assessments, as well as those of many Western experts, exaggerate the scope of Russian-Iranian military and technical cooperation. While Western politicians frequently claim that Russia is "pumping Iran full to capacity" with sophisticated arms, such allegations are far from reality. In analyzing Russian-Iranian military-technical cooperation (MTC), one must take into account the following considerations:

- Up to the 1990s, Iran did not import Russian (Soviet) arms, rather it fully relied on Western arms supplies. Therefore, Russian MTC with Iran is a relatively new endeavor and has been confined to the delivery of arms and equipment. There are relatively few Russian advisors in Iran, and no assistance is provided in developing local arms production.
- Iran has not yet become Russia's principal partner in MTC, and Russian arms have not totally pushed Western weaponry out of Iranian arsenals.
- Arms deliveries are restricted by Russia's national security interests as well as by its regional and international commitments. It is not in Russia's interest to boost Iran's mili-

tary potential to an unstable level of imbalance among the Gulf states.

- Iran's financial capabilities do not enable it to make large-scale arms purchases.
- MTC between Russia and Iran benefits from a favorable political situation: Teheran's foreign policy toward Central Asia and Transcaucasia has shown restraint, and almost no aid has been extended to radical Islamic movements.

Given Russia's loss of many traditional arms markets, including Iraq and Libya, selling military supplies to Iran is of great economic importance. A strategic partnership with Iran is also important politically. Iran is a key neighboring state, and maintaining good relations is vital for protecting Russian national interests along its southern borders. Mutually beneficial arms trade with Iran can promote positive trends in Iran's foreign policy and maintain the regional status quo.

Nevertheless, because of the above-mentioned factors arguing for restraint, Russian arms supplies to Iran are kept at low levels, and the general volume of arms trade will not rise significantly until at least 1998. In the last two or three years, Russian-Iranian military cooperation has intensified within the framework of existing agreements signed prior to the dissolution of the U.S.S.R. In 1993-94, Russia supplied Iran with ten SU-24 aircraft, 150 infantry fighting vehicles, and two diesel submarines (a third one has been prepared for delivery).[16] According to Khalilzad, Russia will also deliver 150 MiG-29 fighters with air-to-air missiles and a large number of SU-24 aircraft with air-to-surface missiles. The agreement of 1989 envisaged the supply of forty-eight MiG-29 aircraft. In 1991 the list was extended to include more MiG-29, MiG-31, SU-24 and, according to some sources, MiG-27 aircraft. Khalilzad alleges that Russia promised to supply Iran with twelve TU-22M long-range bombers.[17] But the Israeli publication *The Middle East Military Balance*, which generally provides detailed data, does not support these figures, acknowledging a transfer of only thirty-five MiG-29s. Other sources suggest that Iran has been supplied with MiG-31 aircraft and continues to retain over a hundred Iraqi military aircraft that defected to its territory during Operation Desert Storm (twelve MiG-23s, four MiG-29s, forty SU-22s, twenty-two SU-24s, seven SU-25s and twenty-four

Mirage G-1s).[18] It is not known how many of those aircraft have actually been integrated into the Iranian air force.

According to *The Middle East Military Balance* 1994 survey, the following Russian weapons and military equipment are in the inventory of the Iranian armed forces.

Army

Small Arms

7.62 mm AK-47 assault rifles and 7.62 mm Degtyarev automatic rifles.

Tanks

T-72: Several hundred ordered

T-62: 150

T-55 / Type 69 / Type 59 (Chinese analogues of T-55)

Armored Vehicles

BMP-1   100

BMP-2: Delivery of several hundred has already started.

BTR 50/60

Artillery

D-30 self-propelled howitzer (with a range of 16 km): Several hundred.

Multiple-launch rockets systems are appearing.

Anti-Tank Missiles

AT-3 Sagger, 500-3000 m, "Malyutka"

AT-5 Sprandel, carried on BMP-2, 3600 m

Air Defense Missiles

SA-6 Gainful, 9M9 "Kub," 3-21 km

SA-7 Grail 9M32 "Strela-2," 3.5 km (apparently NI-5A, a modernized Chinese version of Strela)

Air Force

MiG-29: 35 (including those captured from Iraq)

SU-24: 24 (captured from Iraq)

New orders: MiG-29s, SU-24s and other aircraft

Air-to-Air Missiles

AA-10 Alamo, R-27, 20-34 km

Air-to-Surface Missiles

AS-14 Kedge, KH-29, 30 km

Reports have been received on the following supplies:
AS-1 Kennel, KS-1, 90 km, radar-guided
AS-5 Kelt, KSR-2, 160 km, radar-guided
AS-6 Kingfish, KSR-5, 240 km, inertial guidance
AA-11 Archer, ("air-to-air") 2-73, 39-68 km
Negotiations are under way on AA-12 delivery.

Air Defense Missile Systems
SA-2 Guidelint V-75 "Dvina" (range 34.8 km).
SA-5 Gammen S-200 "Volga" (range 250 km).

Current deliveries include: Six batteries of SA-10 Grumble; S-CII "Buk" (range 70 km); SA-12 Gladiator, S-300 V (range 150 km); as well as SA-5. Delivery of modern air defense command, control, and communication systems has not been confirmed.

Navy
Kilo-class submarines ("Varshavyanka"): Two—with an additional one on order[19]

Iran also imports weapons from Eastern Europe and the Commonwealth of Independent States (CIS)—namely, from the Czech Republic and Slovakia (tanks, radars); Hungary (radars, spare parts for tanks); Ukraine (artillery, tanks); and Poland (tanks). China and North Korea supply Iran with modernized Russian weapons systems and Scud-B and Scud-C missile technology (e.g., SS-1, R-17 or 9E-72). According to some Russian publications, Ukraine has delivered production technology for the T-80 tank to be produced at Iranian military-industrial facilities under the name "Zulfagar."[20] In 1992, Iran reportedly tried to purchase $10 billion worth of arms, military equipment, and technologies in the Commonwealth of Independent States (CIS) to "realize an ambitious re-armament program and expansion of indigenous military production."[21]

Clearly Iran is a strong regional military power. Russian expert Gen. A. I. Gusher numbers the size of the Iranian army, the Revolutionary Guards, and law enforcement agencies at 750,000 men, constituting more than thirty divisions, twenty-five brigades, and twenty air force squadrons. Iran's inventory includes approximately 1,800 tanks, 1,700 armored personnel carriers and infantry fighting vehicles, 6,000 artillery pieces and mortars, 220 combat aircraft, twenty warships, and many other resources. Despite Iran's developing defense relationship with Russia and the West's ban on arms exports to Teheran, Western arms and equipment delivered prior to the Islamic revolution continue to comprise the bulk of the inventory of the Iranian armed forces. Furthermore, the majority of army specialists have been trained in the West. Taking into account constraints existing on both sides, a complete re-equipment with Russian weapons and a re-training of military personnel to operate such equipment is an unlikely possibility in the near future.

Does an Iranian Threat Exist?

The Iranian armed forces are far from recovered from the wounds inflicted by the Islamic revolution. Even a partial re-training of military personnel required by shifting from Western to Eastern weapons would take considerable effort. But Teheran's military potential is likely to change in the coming decade.

Anthony Cordesman, a prominent American expert, devised the following list of situations in which Iran could use or threaten to use its armed forces. Note that this list is exhaustive and that many of these scenarios, such as Iranian interference in conflicts within the CIS, are highly improbable.

- Civil war or armed rebellion in Iran involving religious factors
- Iraqi invasion of Iran
- Spread of the conflict between the Turkish armed forces and Kurdish insurgents into Iranian territory
- Armenian invasion of Azerbaijan escalating into a religious confrontation
- Ethnic and religious conflicts with the secular regimes of Central Asia
- Coup in Bahrain, or Shiite rebellion in Saudi Arabia or another Gulf state
- Crisis in world oil prices, or struggle for oil quotas
- Large-scale armed conflict between Israel and Shiites supported by Iran

- Religious coup or conflict between Islamic and secular authorities in a bordering country
- Military challenge to Iranian sovereignty over the Abu Musa and/or Big and Small Tomb islands
- Air or sea battles in the Gulf over oil rights or sea routes
- Large-scale military conflict between Israel and the Palestinians and/or Syria[22]

Teheran's negative attitude toward negotiating a comprehensive Middle East settlement—in particular its failure to recognize Israel's right to exist—has provoked strong anti-Iranian sentiments in the United States. Nevertheless, Israeli experts on the subject remain skeptical about the credibility of Iran's threats. "Iran poses a limited threat to Israel," according to one prominent expert, Col. Ephraim Kam. "While Iran's support for the main terrorist organisations at war against Israel— Hezbollah and, to a lesser extent, Hamas and Islamic Jihad— intensifies the campaign against Israel, this does not pose any essential threat to the nation's security."[23]

According to Colonel Kam, Iran's stockpiling of conventional arms also poses no serious threat to Israel. Iran is unlikely to take part in any new war against Israel on the side of the Arabs. If a peace treaty is signed between Syria and Israel, Iran's threat to Israel—whether through direct invasion or through organizations like Hezbollah—will diminish further. Only if Iran obtains surface-to-surface missiles within striking range of Israel will a serious threat emerge. Despite the fact that the two countries have never been enemies, the prospect of Iran's becoming a nuclear power is especially feared in Israel. However, Iran would likely consider nuclear weapons as "weapons of last resort" and can be viewed as a responsible state not disposed to military adventures.

Iran did not try to acquire long-range missiles until Iraq's invasion in 1982, when it suffered Frog-7 rocket attacks. The attacks compelled Iran to produce its own Iran-130 and later Shahin-2 missiles.[24] Like Iraq, Iran made a futile attempt to modernize Scuds. Between 1987 and 1992, Iran purchased 200-300 North Korean Scud-B missiles. By 1989 it had acquired 150 to 200 CSS-8 long-range missiles, thirty to thirty-five launchers with a range of 150 km, and guided missile technology from China. Iran discussed its desire to purchase Chinese surface-to-surface missiles: M-9 (range 600 km, payload 600 kg) and M-11 missiles (range 300 km, payload 750-800 kg). North Korea's missile system (already in Iranian hands) has a range of 500-600 km and a payload at least 500 kg.[25] According to Anthony Cordesman, all Iranian missiles could be destroyed by Patriot air defense systems, and the launchers could be annihilated by the U.S. Air Force.[26] Though these weapons are of no real military threat to the Gulf states, their existence exerts certain psychological influence on Iran's neighbors.

Considering the Arab Gulf states to be potential strategic enemies, Iran will continue to amass and modernize its arsenals to keep pace with those states. Teheran will try to benefit from contradictions between anti-Western (Iraq) and pro-Western (Gulf Cooperation Council) sections of the opposing Arab camp and to actively rely on the Shiite factor in the Gulf. Control of the Gulf islands and possession of a submarine fleet do not give Iran any substantial military advantages beyond intimidation and deterrence, and it appears that Iran is not capable of posing a real threat to its neighbors in the future.

Iraq Under Sanctions

The Iraqi arms market boomed in the 1970s and 1980s. In these two decades, Iraq spent over $80 billion on arms. The Soviet Union, France, and West Germany were the most active players in the Iraqi market, with Soviet sales accounting for over 60 percent of the value of all sales.[27] By 1980, technical and economic assistance enabled Iraq to develop a powerful military industry capable of supplying its armed forces with a wide range of locally produced military items, including small arms, artillery, ammunition, chemicals, high explosives, and missiles. The industrial sector utilized German technologies for producing nerve gas, including those of the Carl Colb company. Modernization of Scud missiles benefited from the technology of another German firm, Hawert. In addition to supplying Mirage fighters and Exocet missiles, France set up maintenance and servicing centers for those armaments.

Iraqi nuclear research capabilities were established and modernized with technical and economic assistance from France and the Soviet Union. France delivered two nuclear research reactors, including an Ozirak facility with a complete technical operation cycle. The Soviet Union, in turn, satisfied a significant portion of Iraq's nuclear fuel requirements.

Iraq's invasion of Kuwait in 1991 destroyed the Iraqi market for arms and military technology. A U.N. embargo on military supplies after the Gulf War halted military and economic cooperation with the West and the former Soviet Union. All official channels of arms supplies have been effectively blocked, preventing Iraq from replenishing its war losses in aircraft and armored vehicles. The nuclear program was cancelled; nuclear installations were dismantled; and all nuclear and special materials were returned to their countries of origin, including Russia. By March 1994, Iraq had parted with 547 tons of raw uranium and 50 kg of enriched uranium. Twenty-eight thousand chemical projectiles, warheads, and bombs were liquidated under supervision of the United Nations.[28]

It was only after Iraq's defeat in the Gulf War that the alarmingly rapid development of Baghdad's nuclear weapons program was disclosed to the world community. In accordance with U.N. Security Council Resolution 687, all weapons of mass destruction in Iraq had to be declared, identified, localized, and liquidated, and an appropriate monitoring system had to be established to ensure that Iraq will never create new weapons of mass destruction. It was explicitly prohibited for Iraq to obtain nuclear, biological, and chemical weapons, as well as ballistic missiles with a range exceeding 150 km. After a long period of hard pressure, Iraq yielded to the U.N. demands.

But, as soon as sanctions are lifted, Baghdad surely intends to restore military and economic relations with Russia, its traditional supplier. Iraq continues to suffer from an acute shortage of spare parts for Soviet armaments and military equipment. Russian defense enterprises are also hoping to restore their position in the Iraqi market.

Meanwhile, the West continues to regard Iraq as a serious threat, for all forms of proliferation, as long as Saddam Hussein is in power. In 1993, U.S. Secretary of Defense Les Aspin declared that Iran and Iraq were the most serious threats for the United States in the 1990s.[29] Iraq's military potential was estimated to be: over 380,000 active duty servicemen; 700 tanks; about 4,400 armored vehicles; perhaps 2,000 artillery pieces excluding mortars; about 310 combat aircraft; and more than twenty warships.[30]

Despite the failed invasion of Kuwait, heavy losses, and international sanctions, Iraq's army remains a sound military force. It is considered one of the best in the region, with huge numerical strength and large reserve forces. With its strong corporate mentality, the Iraqi officer corps is the main supporting pillar of the regime—at the same time as it is Saddam Hussein's greatest potential threat. Officers are jealous of the privileged position of the elite units of the Republican Guard, which suffered least in past wars. A powerful repressive system enables Saddam Hussein to subdue the discontent among officers. Saddam also skillfully manipulates public opinion, directing popular discontent against the West for "punishing the whole Iraqi people." This same skill is displayed in taking advantage of the popular fear of a disintegration of the country.

Although in the present situation Iraq cannot be regarded as a serious threat to its neighbors, the underlying motives of its previous aggressive actions remain. Any Iraqi government will recognize that Iraq is left with practically no free access to the sea. In this situation one can hardly expect Iraq to abandon visions of changing the geostrategic situation in the Gulf. Sanctions cannot last indefinitely. Soon enough, Iraq can be expected to restore its military potential.

Some experts admit that Iraq could be involved in even current regional conflicts. Anthony Cordesman considers such a scenario probable, but emphasizes that Iraq's current weakness renders it a second-rate player. The following scenarios of Iraqi involvement in armed conflicts are possible, according to Cordesman.

- Clash with Turkey or Iran after Iraqi attempts to attack the Kurds or, on the contrary, because of Iraqi support to the P.K.K. insurgents
- Medium-intensity conflict with the United States after Iraqi attacks against the Kurds in the Operation Provide Comfort zone in northern Iraq
- Conflict with Iran because of Iraq's attitude toward Shiites and/or an Iranian attack against *Moujaheddin-e-Khalk* armed opposition unit based in Iraqi territory
- Large-scale conflict over Baghdad's failure to allow a U.N.

inspection, violation of closed airspace, or Iraqi attempts to penetrate Kuwait
- Armed clashes following U.S. or U.N. strikes delivered as a reprisal for Iraq's support of terrorism or use of non-conventional weapons
- Act of terrorism using chemical or biological agents
- Use of mines or missiles against U.S. military installations or warships in the Gulf
- Conflict with Syria over a peace agreement with Israel or another reason.[31]

In the near future, however, Iraq will probably refrain from using its military power. The present regime in Baghdad is struggling to survive at the same time that it is seeking to improve its international stature. Nevertheless, an indiscreet and unpredictable Saddam Hussein could again resort to reckless steps that would endanger the region.

When sanctions against Iraq are lifted, the international community must continue to ensure that Saddam Hussein's actions to renew a nuclear program are closely and reliably monitored. Experts believe that, if left without proper controls, Iraq could develop nuclear weapons within a decade. Despite the fact that Iran and Iraq are historical adversaries and that mutual hostility has been fanned by eight years of war in the 1980s, a strategic partnership cannot be excluded. Purely pragmatic considerations, common short-term interests, and shared subjection to sanctions and the U.S. policy of "dual containment" could galvanize such a partnership. In May 1995, Iran seriously attempted a rapprochement when a delegation from its foreign ministry visited Baghdad.

While foreseeing changes in Iran or Iraq is difficult, their sense of vulnerability and isolation from the world community, coupled with the decay of their military hardware, hardly works to promote prudence. Any attempts by Iran, Iraq, or another state in the region to dominate its neighbors would bring about destabilization and should be opposed.

Turkey as a New Exporter

Turkey is developing democratic institutions as a member of NATO, and it is a possible future member of the European Union. Its growing military power and unsettled internal (the

Kurdish minority) and external disputes (problems with Iraq, Syria, Greece, Cyprus, Armenia), as well as its striving for regional influence, are perceived as potentially threatening and destabilizing.

Like Israel, Turkey prefers to obtain modern military technologies from domestic production rather than to purchase arms abroad. According to assessments of the Russian Academy of Sciences, Turkey is 70-80 percent self-sufficient in armaments production (Israel's self-sufficiency has reached 90 percent). While NATO membership has made it easier for Turkey to supply its armed forces with modern weapons, it has imposed certain commitments as well.

The Turkish military and Chief of the Turkish General Staff Ismail Karadayi in particular consider the Middle East arms race a dangerous threat to regional security. Presently, Turkey is modernizing its air force, navy, and ground forces, which consist of four field armies (470,000 active duty servicemen, 800,000 reserves, 3,700 tanks, 3,500 armored vehicles).[32] Turkey pays special attention to building up the capabilities of the 3d Field Army deployed in the northeast of the country. It was the first to get third-generation tanks (German Leopard-1 and I-60A3). Ankara has become increasingly active in the Black Sea. Germany has equipped the Turkish navy with modern missile boats, IEKO-200 T missile frigates, and 1200/1400-type submarines.[33]

Turkey exports armaments as well, even to developed states. According to the Turkish press, the MCC (Machinery and Chemicals Company), which produces a large spectrum of armaments for the Turkish army—from artillery to small arms, as well as ammunition—increased arms exports to $15 million in 1994. Turkey expects arms exports to reach $20 million in 1995.[34] After the Turkish incursion into Iraqi Kurdistan in March 1995, Norway proscribed weapons and military equipment deliveries to Ankara. In reply, Turkey prohibited its companies to enter into contracts with Oslo. Despite these restrictions, exports of Turkish MG-3 machine guns reportedly continued. By May 1995, 5,250 pieces were delivered and 1,000 more were ordered.[35]

Armed skirmishes in the spring of 1995 again proved Turkey's high degree of self-sufficiency. In the future, Turkish authorities will continue "solving" the problem of its Kurdish minority (which constitutes at least one-fourth of the population) by military means. While arms embargoes imposed by a number of countries act as instruments of moral pressure, they unfortunately will hardly change Ankara's determination to resort to force and to reduce the Kurdish problem to a "counter-terrorism" campaign.

Paying special attention to P.K.K. counter-insurgency operations, Turkey has expressed an interest in acquiring Russian armored personnel carriers. Rapidly developing economic cooperation between Russia and Turkey has not, however, removed friction. Possible Russian cooperation with NATO may ease such tensions—in much the same way as NATO membership served to suppress conflict between Turkey and Greece.

The Balkans remain an area of paramount importance to Turkey, despite discord between Athens and Ankara. The membership of both Greece and Turkey in NATO and their strategic parity have worked to promote peace in the region. It is, however, possible to envision conflict scenarios between third countries in which either Greece or Turkey could become involved. A subsequent chain reaction could spread throughout the Middle East. Turkish researchers I. Turan and D. Barlas believe that a civil war in Kosovo between ethnic Albanians and Serbian authorities could ignite such a conflict. Albanian intervention in Kosovo would undoubtedly be followed by intervention by Greece or Macedonia. Should Albania be defeated and partially occupied, Turkey might step in. Another possible scenario is a Serbian armed intervention in Macedonia, possibly accompanied by Greek and Bulgarian actions. Turkey could very possibly interfere in such a scenario as well.[36]

After the collapse of the bipolar system, peace in the Balkans has become less secure. In Turkey's perspective, a balance among regional adversaries can now be easily broken. A similar situation seems to prevail in the Middle East. Thus, despite its present role as a bulwark in the regional strategic balance, under certain situations, Turkey could still become involved in armed conflict.

The Gulf Cooperation Council: Relying on Foreign Powers

Members of the Gulf Cooperation Council (GCC) have already accumulated copious amounts of modern arms, principally from the United States and Western Europe. In 1994, for example, the Saudi Arabian air force had 270 combat aircraft, including ninety-two U.S. F-15 C/D Eagle, twenty-four Tornado ADV, and forty-seven multi-purpose Tornado IDS. Forty-eight more Tornado IDS were ordered for delivery in 1995-98. Other forthcoming deliveries include seventy-two to seventy-five F-15S fighters, 108 cargo aircraft, 171 helicopters, and five AWACS aircraft. Saudi Arabia also has access to modern missile technology. In 1994, six MIM-104 Patriot air defense systems were in active duty with more on order, together with seventeen MIM-23A upgraded Hawk systems. Saudi Arabia's navy consists of more than eighty modern warships.

In 1994, the Saudi Royal Army had 700 tanks (American I-60AC and French AIO-30). In addition to that, 315 I-1A2 tanks were acquired, and an order for another 150 tanks is planned. The Saudi army, navy, and air force total 126,000-136,000 troops, about 30,000 *mujaheddin* (volunteers supporting the National Guard) and 10,000-15,000 border guards. As their numerical strength grows, Saudi armed forces are being reorganized. The monarchy has charted an ambitious military modernization plan aimed at a twofold increase of the army ranks.[37] In contrast with Saudi Arabia, the armed forces of the other members of the GCC have as their top priority the development of modern air defense systems. Neighboring Kuwait, for instance, purchased five U.S. Patriot batteries and twelve Russian surface-to-air systems.

As for the Kuwaiti arms market, the outcome of Desert Storm stimulated a rash of buying. The armed forces needed to recover from significant depletion in weapons and loss of military equipment and to repair military infrastructure, of which 80 percent had been destroyed. In an attempt to soften competition, the United States, the United Kingdom, and France agreed to divide up the Kuwaiti arms market: American companies would supply weapons for the Kuwaiti air force and air defense; British companies, arms for the ground forces; and French companies, navigational and other technical facilities for the navy. In 1994, that arrangement enabled the United States to supply Kuwait with twelve out of forty F-18 fighters, five Patriot systems, and 210 Patriot missiles worth over $1 billion. A $4-billion contract was signed to deliver 250 American I1A2 tanks. Britain won contracts to deliver 300 Warrior infantry fighting vehicles worth $1.5 billion. French companies, for their part, signed a contract to deliver a mere dozen 155 mm self-propelled artillery pieces.[38] United Arab Emirates, however, continues to receive French Leclerc tanks (436 were ordered) and Mirage-2000 aircraft.

The United States has concluded a technical and economic agreement with GCC members to establish common air defenses, including an AWACS-based early warning system. The cost of procuring four E-3A AWACS airplanes is around $5 billion. Washington's leading position in the Middle East arms market has been strengthened further by bilateral defense agreements and military cooperation. Enhancing the land components of the air defense system alone (including the purchase of 700 Patriot missiles) cost the Saudis about $3 billion.[39]

While Russia continues to offer its arms and equipment to the countries in the Gulf, it has not achieved much success. Its first large contracts were signed with Kuwait and United Arab Emirates for the supply of S-300 air defense missile systems, Smerch multiple-launch rocket systems, and infantry fighting vehicles. At the same time and in accordance with existing agreements, Russia will deliver about 100 combat aircraft to Syria, including fourteen SU-17s, thirty SU-24s, and fifty MiG-29s, as well as ten surface-to-air missile launchers designed to destroy various targets, including operational and tactical missiles.

Indigenous production in the Gulf is developing slowly, but for the most part the GCC states rely on imports of modern weapons and military equipment. This approach makes the Gulf states highly dependent on large-scale arms purchases to satisfy their national defense requirements. As previously noted, however, they do not count exclusively on their own defense forces but anticipate Western military deployments in case of a foreign invasion. In 1991-92, Kuwait agreed to establish facilities for deploying several U.S. army brigades on its territory and consented to joint military maneuvers. By 1993, Kuwait could accommodate a brigade with 110 tanks. A similar decision was taken by Qatar. If the same kind of agreement is reached with the U.A.E., then the United States could deploy army divisions in the Gulf wherever necessary.

The GCC states consider Iran and Iraq to be major external threats. From Israel's perspective, all Arab states seem to go out of their way to narrow the gap between military potentials (Israel's missile potential prevails). Over a hundred Israeli Jerico-2 ballistic missiles (range 1500 km, payload 650 kg) as well as Israeli satellites are perceived as a threat by Arab states. Experts believe that the Shavit satellite booster—if adapted to accommodate a warhead—can increase the missile range to 7,000 km.[40] The excessive military expenses of the Gulf Cooperation Council members heavily burden their budgets and promote internal tensions. Despite vast financial resources, they have become debtors to industrially developed states. Kuwait alone owes out $40 billion.

Conclusions

Positive processes are taking place in the Middle East: The Arab-Israeli conflict is subsiding; weapons of mass destruction are being liquidated; non-proliferation regimes are becoming tougher; international cooperation is developing; and guidelines for deterring potential aggressors are being established. Parallel to these developments, however, is the negative potential of uncontrolled stockpiling of conventional weapons. Moreover, isolating Iran and Iraq works against transforming the Middle East into a region of peace and stability.

Along with the restriction of arms deliveries and harsh verification measures, the time is ripe to establish a collective security system in the Middle East. However, it will be impossible to maintain regional peace and stability without the participation of key states such as Iran and Iraq. The creation of a regional security system involving the leading world powers could help to fix quotas for conventional armaments, taking into account legitimate defense requirements.

The international community might promote a negotiation process involving all states in the Middle East, seek regional confidence-building measures, and work toward greater transparency in arms transfers. The first steps toward disarmament and confidence-building measures in the Middle East were taken in 1992-93 in the framework of the Arab-Israeli settlement. The Arms Control and Regional Security (ACRS) working group, created at an international conference in Moscow, included Israel and twelve Arab states, among them Egypt, Jordan, Saudi Arabia, Oman, U.A.E., Morocco, Algeria, and Tunisia. Palestine joined in 1993. The group worked with only limited success. Egypt insisted on making the Middle East a zone free from nuclear, biological, and chemical weapons (NBC-free), which was resolutely opposed by Israel. On the other hand, Israel stressed conventional arms disparities among the Middle East's armies, noting that deep mutual suspicions and huge conventional arsenals constitute the main obstacles to reducing regional confrontation. Israel insisted on two preconditions before creating a NBC-free zone in the Middle East: the attainment of a comprehensive peace and the adoption of mutual verification measures. A proposal was made to use the past Soviet-American arms control experience; the parties decided not to rely on international verification agencies, but to develop mutually acceptable national procedures of control among themselves.

As the talks proceeded, national positions started to converge, and the working group drafted a declaration on common principles in 1994. However, the absence of Syria, Iran, Iraq, and Libya reduced its value, and some states, for example Saudi Arabia, belittled the value of the talks. Israeli experts believe that, in a conventional war, Israel would have an advantage over its Arab neighbors. At the same time, however, the Arab nations have the capability to hit Israel's rear with ballistic missiles. "Thus, both sides refrain from a first strike and from a full use of their advantages."[41]

For monitoring the proliferation of conventional armaments, one can hardly rely on the good will of Middle East arms importers. A decisive role can be played best by the suppliers, who should agree on arms sales control mechanisms. However, the financial incentives offered by the oil-producing states tend to temper any consideration of self-restraint. Like Western oil importers, Russia seeks a stable and secure Middle East. It is in favor of mutual understanding and cooperation with the United States and Western Europe and seeks better relations with the GCC. However, restrictive measures taken against Iran and Iraq, who both have been Russia's traditional strategic partners, are deemed by many in Russia as "punishment of the people for their leaders."[42] This is not regarded as acceptable to Russia.

Collective international efforts are needed to maintain the fragile peace in the Middle East. However, acute contradictions between key nations of the region and different approaches to those nations by the leading world powers make the attainment of this goal problematic, at least in the short-term.

Notes

[1]U.S. Library of Congress, *Conventional Arms Transfers to Developing Nations (1998-1995)*, August 15, 1996, 23.

[2]*Krasnaya Zvezda, April 7, 1995.*

[3]*Finansovye Izvestia*, March 28, 1995.

[4]*Atlas, No.15, October 14, 1993.*

[5]*Compass*, 1993, No.96, 44-5.

[6]*Izvestia, April 12, 1995.*

[7]*International Atomic Energy Agency (IAEA) Press Release 92/11, February 14, 1992.*

[8]*Testimony before U.S. Senate Governmental Affairs Committee, February 24, 1993.*

[9]*Izvestia*, April 12, 1995.

[10]Izvestia, *April 18, 1995.*

[11]*Wall Street Journal*, April 20, 1995.

[12]Extract from V. E. Novikov's presentation at the Russian-Iranian roundtable organized by the Russian Center for Strategic and International Studies and the Institute of Political and International Studies of Iran, Moscow, October 4-5, 1995.

[13]See the 1995 Report of the Russian Foreign Intelligence Service: *Sluzhba Vneshney Razvedki Rossiyskoy Federatsii. Dogovor o nerasprostranenii yadernogo oruzhiya: Problemy prodleniya*. Moscow, 1995, 23-25.

[14]Data from the presentation by Russian MOD expert Maj. Gen. (retired) A. I. Gusher at the Russian-Iranian roundtable, October 4-5, 1995.\

[15]Zalmay Khalilzad. "The United States and the Persian Gulf: Preventing Regional Hegemony," *Survival*. Summer 1995, 99.

[16]*Atlas*, No.37, September 16, 1994.

[17]Khalilzad, op. cit., 17, 100.

[18]*The Middle East Military Balance*, Jerusalem Post and Westview Press, 1994, 281-97.

[19]Ibid.

[20]*Compass*, Moscow, September 1994.

[21]*Izvestia*, November 26, 1992.

[22]Anthony Cordesman. *Iran and Iraq: The Military Dimensions of Possible Regional Conflict*, Woodrow Wilson Center, 89.

[23]Ephraim Kam. "The Iranian Threat," *The Middle East Military Balance*, 1993-1994.

[24]W. Seth Carus and Joseph S. Bermudez. "Iran's Growing Missile Forces." *Jane's Defence Weekly*, July 23, 1988, 126-31.

[25]Cordesman, op.cit., 42-43.

[26]Ibid.

[27]*Defense Journal*, No.9, 1990, 23.

[28]*Izvestia*, February 15, 1994; April 5, 1994.

[29]*The Bottom Up Review: Forces for a New Era*. Department of Defense. September 1, 1993.

[30]*The Middle East Military Balance*, 163.

[31]Cordesman, 90.

[32]Krasnaya Zvezda, *March 15, 1995*.

[33]*Ibid.*

[34]*Turkish Daily News*, Ankara, May 24, 1995.

[35]Ibid.

[36]Ilter Turan and Dilek Barlas. "Turkey and the Balkans: Searching for Stability. Koc University." Working Paper No.1995/02, 18.

[37]The Middle East Military Balance, *410-25*.

[38]*Zarubezhnoye Voyennoye Obozreniye*, No.4, 1994.

[39]Keyhan International, December 2, 1992.

[40]SIPRI Yearbook 1993, *250*.

[41]*The Middle East Military Balance*, 163.

[42]Cordesman, 91.

Chapter 6
An Uneasy Partnership: Sino-Russian Defense Cooperation and Arms Sales

Pavel Felgengauer

From as early as the siege of the Albazinsky Ostrog by the Manchurian Chinese in 1685-86 and the Nerchinsk peace treaty that followed in 1689, Sino-Russian relations have developed under the influence of two conflicting factors: on the one hand, advantages from peaceful business relations, and on the other hand, enmity and mutual suspicion emanating from each empire's long-standing desire to dominate Central Asia and the Pacific.

Russian merchants have always benefited from trade with China. Strange as it may seem, the composition of exports and imports has scarcely changed since the 17th and 18th centuries, consisting primarily of tea, textiles, metals, medical herbs, and other natural components of traditional Chinese medicine. Weapons and arms production technology have also been a traditional item of exchange, especially in the 20th century, when the Soviet Union supported with arms first the Kuomintang (Chinese nationalists) and then local Communists and the People's Liberation Army (PLA) of China.

In the 1950s (during the Moscow-Peking axis), Soviet assistance enabled mainland China to develop a "modern" military-production industry. Since then, the PLA and the Chinese air force have been equipped predominantly with Soviet-type arms, basically indigenous clones or modifications. These items included J-5, J-6, and J-7 fighters (analogues of the Soviet MiG-17 and MiG-19); T-59 and T-69 tanks fashioned from the old Soviet T-54; and air missile-defense systems of the famous S-75 family. Small arms—such as the Kalashnikov assault rifle, DShK heavy machine guns, and various Soviet rifles and carbines—were also routinely reproduced in China.

In exchange for arms and technology, China has supplied the U.S.S.R. with textiles, thermoses, apples, and tea. This arrangement lasted until the sharp deterioration of bilateral relations in the early 1960s. The period of friendly exchanges gave way to a long spell of hostility and preparations for a war which, fortunately, has yet to break out. Even after the Sino-Soviet split, China's military-industry complex continued to operate quite successfully. The Chinese not only supplied their own armed forces but also became active suppliers of cheap clones of Soviet military equipment for the world market—in direct competition with the U.S.S.R. and the West. At the same time, Beijing's breakup with Moscow brought some favors from the West. Launched in 1978, Deng Xiaoping's economic reform program attracted billions of dollars of foreign investment to China and afforded access to Western and Japanese technologies.

Technological cooperation with the West, however, has only marginally benefited the PLA. While the army acquired some new arms, namely TOW, Milan, and HOT anti-tank guided missiles, a strategic reorientation with Western armaments has not occurred. Currently, the PLA has just thirty 155 mm Western artillery pieces compared to over 7,400 items of Soviet artillery, including 122 mm, 152 mm, and self-propelled systems.[1] Despite the efforts of influential figures such as U.S. National Security Advisor Zbigniew Brzezinski to play the "China card"—thereby exerting military pressure on the U.S.S.R.—the West was cautious about supplying Chinese Communists with modern defense technology. The People's Republic of China (PRC) lacked money for direct purchases of Western arms. A handful of modern weapons could not dramatically change the "peasant" nature of the PLA. Moreover, since the bloody clash between the army and students in 1989 at Tiananmen Square, many programs of military cooperation between China and the West have been terminated. Recently, some military cooperation with the United States has resumed.

Over two and a half decades of bitter confrontation with the Soviet Union, China managed to create its own independent strategic missile and tactical nuclear weapons capabilities, which, although not yet equal to those of Britain and France, is clearly of great concern to Russia. At present, China has the following nuclear systems on standby combat duty: four intercontinental strategic missiles carrying five megaton warheads (with a range of up to 13,000 km), up to twenty strategic missiles with a range of 5,000 km, over sixty operational-tactical ballistic missiles; and at least one nuclear submarine with twelve ballistic missiles on board.[2]

However, the Chinese apparently failed to find resources and capabilities for developing a new generation of conventional arms. Military production facilities built with Soviet help are aging, and the export potential of Chinese armaments is shrinking. For China, the best solution is to gain cheap access to modern military and dual-use technologies in exchange for consumer goods—similar to exchange patterns of the 1950s. Most feasible, given the existing Chinese military-industrial potential, has been a continuity of technological "exchange" with Russia—its old friend, enemy, and competitor. External factors have aided this development: In the early 1990s, at the same time that China searched for new sources of advanced technologies, a period of conflict with Russia was replaced by a period of intensive trade and cooperation.

A Buyer and a Seller Find Each Other

In the late 1980s, with the advent of glasnost and "new thinking," twenty-five years of Sino-Soviet confrontation ended. An intensive cross-border movement of both people and goods was renewed. Organized and unorganized (so-called "shuttle") trade turnover increased annually, in particular after the disintegration of the U.S.S.R. in 1991. Cheap Chinese goods, often of poor quality, enjoyed seemingly unlimited demand. Chinese officials soon realized that if individuals could get valuable raw materials, high-quality optics, and cameras in exchange for textiles, footwear, and foodstuffs, the same commercial methods could be applied to arms and military technologies.

From 1980 to 1991, China's GNP grew at an annual rate of 9.4 percent. In the first half of the 1990s, the annual growth rate peaked at 13 percent.[3] The Chinese military budget expanded accordingly, doubling within five years (1990-95).[4] It should be noted, however, that this increase is partly exaggerated due to marked inflation and devaluation of China's national currency.

Because an overheated economy cannot afford significant research and development projects, China canceled or suspended a number of arms modernization programs. Presently the PLA has over fifty J-7 fighters, modeled on the Soviet MiG-21 and successfully launched into serial production in the 1960s. However, China failed to put its more modern J-8 fighter into stable mass production. The military has just over 100 of these, but they have different modifications. In 1990, further modernization activities for the J-8 fighter were suspended.[5] The prospective H-7 bomber with Rolls-Royce Spey 202 engines, which—unlike other Chinese combat airplanes—had no Soviet analogue, had only reached the prototype stage when work ceased. The H-7 was to replace the old H-6 bomber created on the basis of the Soviet TU-16.

In the early 1990s, the Chinese defense industry continued to lag behind its Western counterparts. Chinese authorities regarded the situation as critical when it became clear that the PLA would be ill-prepared to fight in the air and on the seas—whether against the armies of leading industrialized nations, or even against its East Asian neighbors. In contrast, dynamic economic growth permitted many states in Southeast Asia to purchase advanced weaponry from the West. It is with those same countries that China had, and continues to have, territorial and other disputes.

In 1989, top-level Sino-Soviet negotiations were held for the first time in many years. They paved the way for military contacts, military-technical cooperation, talks on border issues, and a reduction in the level of bilateral military tension. These contacts resumed in June 1990 and were quickly followed by mutual examination of the possibility of resuming Soviet arms deliveries to China; they were not discontinued with the disintegration of the U.S.S.R. The visit to China of First Deputy Minister of Defense of the Russian Federation Andrei Kokoshin in October 1992 was crowned by the signing of an agreement on military-technical cooperation. In December of the same year, the first Sino-Russian summit took place. An agreement on the demarcation of the eastern border shared by Russia and China was signed during a visit to Moscow by the Secretary General of the Chinese Communist Party in May 1991 and ratified by both sides in 1992. An agreement on the western sector of the border (with the participation of Kazakhstan, Kyrgyzstan, and Tajikistan) was signed during the second visit of the Chinese Secretary General in September 1994.

Ironically, local authorities in the Far East and Trans-Baikal areas resisted final settlement of all border disputes with China, since it would have led to troop withdrawals and a reduction in military garrisons—with the consequent loss of many jobs. Moscow's intention to promote strategic cooperation and partnership with Beijing has gradually overcome the influence of parochial interests. Meanwhile, Russia and China have attempted to relax military tensions along their borders and have agreed on a number of additional confidence-building measures.

Since 1992, Russian and Chinese military officials have maintained continuous contact at various levels. During a July 1994 visit to Moscow, China's defense minister to Russia signed an agreement on preventing dangerous military activities; the parties also agreed to coordinate technical procedures on settling border incidents.

Nevertheless, Russia and China have yet to become allies or strategic partners. Their military cooperation continues to be a function of trade in arms and military technology. Russian military contracts with China presently include commitments by the Russian defense ministry to train Chinese pilots, land technicians, and weapons-system operators at Russian test fields and in Russian military schools. Russian military personnel also train and educate Chinese experts in handling Russian military equipment on PRC territory. These contracts generate significant revenue for the Russian armed forces. It was not mere coincidence, therefore, that the most enthusiastic support of developing cooperation with China and its forces came from the Russian air force and its commander-in-chief, Gen. Peter Deinekin.

China's strong desire for Russian military equipment coincided with equally strong pressure by Russian arms manufacturers to sell their products to any and all interested parties. In 1992, the reformist government of Gaidar and Burbulis drastically cut Russia's defense budget. The Ministry of Defense and the General Staff subsequently cut acquisitions of new equipment as well as research and development programs. The supposed unity of the powerful Russian military-industrial complex was an illusion. Faced with a choice between spending very limited resources on new equipment or saving a maximum number of divisions, Russian military officials unhesitatingly chose the latter option.

Of course, some weapons were still ordered for the troops and received, but no one agreed to pay, under the pretext of insufficient budget allocations. On several occasions between 1992 and 1996, the Russian government took specific measures to pay its debts to defense manufacturers, but the overall amount owed by the government to defense enterprises swelled to over 11 trillion rubles by the end of 1995. Facing such a desperate situation, exports became the last hope of Russian arms producers.

In the 1980s, according to data provided to the author in 1992 by a deputy in the Ministry of Foreign Economic Relations, the U.S.S.R. exported enormous amounts of armaments. It annually exported weapons and military equipment worth about 12-13 billion "foreign currency rubles" (roughly US $20 billion, according to the official rate of 1 FCR = $1.6). Record results were achieved in 1989, when arms exports reached 14.5 billion FCR ($23 billion). These data are not in complete accord with those published by the Stockholm International Peace Research Institute (SIPRI). It is necessary, however, to bear in mind that a "foreign currency ruble" is a calculation unit, and therefore delivery volumes expressed in FCR cannot reflect actual revenues since grants were also included in those figures. In particular, in the same year (1989) the volume of grants reached 2 billion FCR (about $3 billion) and credit supplies amounted to 9 billion FCR ($14.5 billion). Most of those credits have never been returned.

Soviet arms exports in the 1980s were substantial, totaling 130 billion FCR. Moreover, according to the same source, 50 billion of these ($80 billion) were compensated in the same decade by money payments and supplies of commodities, including, for example, Iraqi crude oil. Naturally enough, the stunning commercial success of Soviet arms traders in the 1980s was stimulated by a very specific international situation: the war between

Iran and Iraq. The United States placed an arms embargo on both of these nations, and this created an unprecedented demand for Soviet-made arms. Currently, such "favorable" circumstances are nowhere to be seen. Nonetheless, figures in the military-industrial complex still cling to the image of a "golden age" of Russian arms exports that could be brought back with enough effort.

Many Russian arms manufacturers expected an export boom in 1992, when some analysts assured them of high global market demand for their products. This opinion was most persistently expressed by Mikhail Malei, former adviser to President Yeltsin on defense conversion. At that particular moment, China became a principal target of the Russian arms marketing campaign toward "non-traditional" geographic areas. In 1992, twenty-six SU-27 and SU-27UB fighters were delivered to China. According to the Russian Ministry of Foreign Economic Relations, the overall value of the contract, taking into account all accompanying armaments (air-to-air guided missiles, etc.) as well as education and training of Chinese pilots and technicians, reached $1.4 billion.

These new air-superiority fighters have tilted the balance of power in the Western Pacific in favor of China, whose armed forces have gained distinctly new capabilities. In summer 1993, the Chinese deputy defense attache in Moscow told the author: "Some time ago we did not have an airplane that could dominate the airspace over the South China Sea (the Spratly Islands, etc.). Now we do have such planes. And that is just fine."

Both parties tried to further develop the initial success of their defense cooperation. In 1993, China held a secret exhibition of Russian military equipment. The exhibition included a live demonstration (on a test field) of many modern systems, including N-300 PMU-1 air defense complexes, Smerch multiple-launch rocket system (MLRS), and others.

The achievements of the Russian military-industrial complex impressed the Chinese. The SU-27 contract was followed by other strategically important contracts to supply China with new armaments, such as "noiseless" Kilo-class diesel submarines (alternative names include Varshavyanka or Project 877) and modern "strategic" N-300 PMU-1 long-range air defense systems (manufactured by NPO Almaz).

The Chinese also contracted Russian design agencies to develop a number of projects for them. Splav GNPP has developed a Chinese version of Smerch MLRS. In 1992, the aircraft design facility in the city of Irkutsk developed a two-seat SU-30 fighter-bomber for China on the basis of a SU-27UB two-seat training aircraft. In May 1994, St. Petersburg's TSNIIGidropribor signed a contract in Beijing to develop a new torpedo for the Chinese navy. The director of TSNIIGidropribor did not mask his jubilant mood in his remark that the "contract virtually saved us."

Agreements on dual-use items have also been signed and implemented since 1992. Of greatest importance is an agreement between the Ministry of Atomic Energy (MINATOM) and China to develop a centrifugal uranium enrichment plant designed in Tomsk-7 (a closed city in Seversk). On January 8, 1995, a Russian-Iranian protocol was signed in Teheran, which, among other things stressed an intention "to prepare a contract on building a uranium mine in Iran, whereupon to conduct negotiations on signing a contract on the construction of a centrifugal uranium enrichment plant on conditions similar to the terms of contracts signed by Russian organizations with companies of third countries." When the author asked Valeri Bogdan, special assistant of the Russian minister of nuclear energy, what exactly "third countries" meant in the Russian-Iranian protocol, his answer was brief: "China." Specific terms of the Russian-Chinese uranium contract remain confidential.

A centrifugal enrichment plant in China might not change the PRC's strategic potential in any event. Previously, the Chinese obtained enriched uranium for nuclear reactors and weapons-grade uranium for warheads by means of an expensive and wasteful gas diffusion method. Now the PRC has more efficient technology for the uranium enrichment process.

Various sources provide different assessments of the overall value of Russian arms transfers to China in the first half of the 1990s. Some experts refer to President Yeltsin, who said that even in 1992 the value of deliveries reached $1.8 billion.[6] However, speaking at the Congress of People's Deputies, Premier Yegor Gaidar mentioned the value of deliveries in 1992 as being only $1 billion. Foreign experts estimate the total amount in 1991-94 to be in the range of $4.5-$6 billion.[7]

Table 4

Russian Arms Trade with China (unofficial data)

Year	Value of Supplies (*millions US dollars*)
1991	$0
1992	$950
1993	$360
1994	$300
1995	$650

Sources in state-run Rosvooruzheniye and the State Committee on Military-Technical Policy rely on modest figures, which generally agree with those of Premier Gaidar. According to those sources, the volume of Russian arms transfers to China has been as shown in Table 4.

The grand total over this period has amounted to some $2,260 million. The data include only paid deliveries and not signed agreements or dual-use technologies such as nuclear technology.

An outside observer would regard the "military-technical partnership" between Russia and China since 1992 as a highly successful example of cooperation between two previously hostile countries in the post–Cold War era. It may seem surprising, therefore, that the majority of Russian arms manufacturers who fulfill Chinese orders are far from delighted with the terms and conditions of this trade.

Tanks and Airplanes Exchanged for Canned Meat, Vodka, and Shoes

Beijing has limited hard-currency reserves to purchase weapons and chose Russia as its main source of modern arms in an attempt to save money. The expectations within the Russian military-industrial complex were quite opposite. Russian industrialists anticipated cash from an avalanche of generous orders. As a result, neither side fully realized its goals, which has produced tensions.

The first serious disillusionment came in 1992—after the first large deal, the SU-27 contract. Of the about $1.4 billion cost, certainly a generous price for twenty-six fighters, only 25 percent was paid in hard currency. The rest was compensated for with consumer goods, including shoes, jackets, canned meat, and vodka.

At the time the contract was signed, the arrangement appeared equitable and advantageous to Russia, whose economy was overwhelmed by barter trade. Money, especially in the form of bank deposits, had less immediate value than consumer goods, which could be exchanged on barter terms for resources.

Thousands upon thousands of private "shuttle traders" flooded Russian cities with Chinese jackets and other goods, earning fortunes within months. Officials in the Ministry of Foreign Economic Relations and directors of military enterprises hoped to achieve the same kind of commercial success by exchanging Chinese commodities for weapons, especially when assembled from "free" components and mobilization resources accumulated during the Cold War.

However, the economic reforms of the Gaidar-Burbulis government again buried the hopes of arms manufacturers. In 1992-93, when cargo trains loaded with Chinese consumer goods began arriving, the situation in the Russian domestic market was fundamentally different. Acute shortages of consumer goods became a thing of the past; shops were full, consumers had many choices, the difference between cash and non-cash rubles nearly disappeared (bank commissions fell below 1.5 percent), and the share of barter deals plummeted. But shipments of consumer goods to military plants continued, and managers did not know what to do with them. In the infant market economy, "shuttle traders" had a competitive edge over the inflexible military giants.

The first enterprise to face this problem was the aircraft plant in Komsomolsk-on-the-Amur, a major participant of the SU-27 contract (SU-27UB fighters were assembled in Irkutsk). The enterprise management distributed as many shoes and meat cans to workers as they could take, but commercial sales were limited because the Russian Far East was already filled to capacity with the same commodities.

Russia did its best to reduce the share of barter deals in their ongoing discussions with the Chinese, to little avail. At a conference of Russian military industry leaders held by Rosvooruzheniye in June 1994, Nikolai Zharkov, director of the Red Sormovo shipyard (which had won a Chinese order to build two Varshavyanka diesel submarines), said in an interview with the author: "The Chinese fooled Alexander Shokhin (a top Russian negotiator). Sixty-five percent of the cost of Kilo-class submarines, a $100 million contract, will be paid for in sneakers or sandals that fall apart in one month's time."

The terms of Russian-Chinese contracts impose harsh limits on the spectrum of goods- for-barter deals. The Chinese selected several large companies as intermediaries, and all barter trade between Moscow and Beijing must go through this official channel, where the choice of goods is rather limited. Apart from Russia, China most likely had a limited market for those goods. A private Russian trader in the business of freight and overseas trade told the author that he once offered the director of Red Sormovo to exchange the Chinese commodities received from the submarine contract for seafood. The trader promised to sell the goods abroad, obviating importation to Russia, and then to transfer hard currency into the bank account of Red Sormovo. The scheme, no matter how reasonable it looked, was not realized. Chinese leaders do not need competitors in operations with exported goods.

Under pressure from Moscow, the share of barter deliveries in military-technical deals has decreased to 50 percent. Moreover, all research and development projects must be paid for in hard currency. But the problem did not disappear; indeed, when the terms of trade became less advantageous for the PRC, it reduced military agreement orders and even cancelled certain projects. One project cancellation was a new two-seater SU-30 fighter-bomber created for China in 1992. Unlike earlier versions of the SU-27, the SU-30 possessed air-refueling capability. Additionally, air-to-ground combat capabilities have been enhanced with additional pylons for armaments and a second crew member to navigate. Moscow expected that China would naturally wish to acquire Russian air-refueling technology along with the SU-30. This particular project failed, however, when China refused to buy an export version of the SU-30.

China needs transfers of the most advanced military technology to modernize its military-industrial complex, as opposed to large-scale acquisitions of the "export versions" of conventional arms. However, the prospect of mass-production of the most modern Russian weapons in China has strong opponents in Russia. This situation would unnecessarily augment competition against Russia's own arms export share and could pose a credible threat to Russian national security.

Moscow-Beijing: A Difficult Partnership

Still in the grip of a deep crisis, the leaders of the Russian military-industrial complex have since 1992 emphatically demanded complete commercial freedom to sell on the world market in order to avoid closures and sustain jobs. In short, the majority of manufacturers are prepared to sell anything to anyone. The reasoning they frequently articulate is: "Why keep existing armaments and weapons technology secret if new and more efficient prototypes are currently available for the Russian army?" The best way to protect Russia's national interests, according to this group, is to safeguard Russia's modern, independent military industry and the system of design agencies (KB), even if survival hangs on exporting the existing know-how and products.

Naturally, designers and directors are not afraid that such a "sellout" could compel Russia to rearm its own forces with a new generation of super-weapons, for this would result in the military-industrial complex again receiving funds for research and development and huge government orders for mass production of new arms. Despite the fact that this technology exists only on the drawing boards or in experimental samples, and the certainty that a strategic rearmament would be costly, these defense industrialists accuse government agencies, Rosvooruzheniye, and especially the Ministry of Defense Commission on Export Control (CEC) of unreasonable behavior, paranoia, and treason. This has resulted in approval delays on lucrative export deals and even cancellation of contracts.

The CEC (which includes MOD officials, representatives of the Foreign Ministry, and intelligence/counter-intelligence experts) has suspended a number of deals, including some with

China, as harmful to the national interests of the Russian Federation. "Our defense industry is presently driven into the corner and has to fight for its mere survival," quotes Andrei Kokoshin, CEC chairman and First Deputy Minister of Defense, in an interview with this author. "Attempts to bypass legislation and sell products in the world market without proper authorization have already been made. According to conventional wisdom, arms exports can rescue the military-industrial complex, and the country as a whole. Some estimate that arms exports earn over $10 billion a year. These are misconceptions."

Occasionally, attempts are made to export recent systems disguised as obsolete ones. Illegal exports of electronic equipment and materials with specially tailored characteristics have taken place. The Ministry of Defense and Russian special services are not, however, in a position to say exactly what was exported, especially in 1992 when operations proceeded without any controls. According to the MOD, arms deliveries were not extensive because of the cost and difficulty of concealment. Rather, the "export" of technological documentation and know-how likely occurred during tours of China by Russian military and industrial experts. Apparently, several important military technology secrets were sold and revealed in this way. China will continue to probe for Russian military secrets as long as Beijing seeks to rearm its forces with a new generation of weapons.

For these reasons, the CEC forwards all prospective contracts to a special service for analysis. The CEC is particularly wary of transfers involving military technology. According to Andrei Kokoshin, the CEC has turned into a "miniature Russian COCOM." Pressures from general managers and designers often compel representatives of the Ministry of Defense and security services to resort to time-tested bureaucratic methods to delay approval of contracts until such time as the parties lose interest in each other.[8]

Russian arms manufacturers have confirmed reports of Chinese intelligence successes in Russia. Red Sormovo Director Nikolai Zharkov recently recounted to the author that the Chinese had obtained classified documentation on Varshavyanka submarines—a modified model earmarked for the Russian navy, which is substantially different from Project 877 (the export version) delivered to Poland, Romania, Algeria, and India. Now, the PRC is demanding that its Kilo-class submarines have the same characteristics.

Moscow-Beijing: Future Prospects

Five years of intensive Sino-Russian military-technical cooperation have led to mutual disillusionment. Both parties clearly expected to get more out of the relationship, yet each country eventually resorted to chicanery and deception, accusing the other of unfair practices. Furthermore, the PLA has yet to become a "modern" army. Thus far, the equipment sold to China does not rank among the best in the Russian inventory. Kilo-class submarines have been in production for well over a decade; SU-27 fighters are even older. According to Zharkov, Varshavyanka diesel submarines are obsolete and too large for the coastal areas of Southeast Asian seas. Germany, for example, offers a similar diesel submarine that is half the size. Four Kilo-class submarines ordered by China were assembled in Nizhny Novgorod and St. Petersburg from spare parts that were remnants from the Soviet era. Zharkov claims that producing Varshavyanka submarines involved the joint effort of all fifteen republics of the former Soviet Union. After honoring the Chinese contract, the project was killed. Now, Russia hopes to launch production of a smaller Lada diesel submarine fabricated solely in Russia. The export version will likely retain the renowned "Kilo-class" catch phrase. Russia does not want to enhance the combat capabilities of the Chinese army to the extent that the PRC could pose a serious threat to Russia's far eastern borders.

Barring major upheavals in world affairs, Moscow and Beijing will continue military-technical cooperation at approximately the present level. Ironically, intelligence gains were not tremendously helpful for the Chinese army because the most modern conventional arms are much more complex than models developed in the 1950s. It is far more difficult today to clone weapon systems from drawings and samples, especially when the production capabilities of components remain limited.

In Russia, the debate between enthusiasts of close military-technical cooperation with China and the skeptics who call for self-restraint will continue, perhaps even escalate into full-scale bureaucratic duels. If by early in the next century Russia still lacks sufficient resources to upgrade its arsenal or to maintain a technological edge over the PLA, then the skeptics are likely to win out. Arms manufacturers will attempt to obtain new contracts to barter weapons for low quality goods, but enthusiasm for this arrangement has cooled, given the unusually strict importation requirements of Chinese officials. At the same time, the Russian military, and especially the General Staff, are opposed to unrestrained exports of the most modern Russian weapons. Various Russian special services support the military's view.

Moreover, the relationship is asymmetrical. China is generally on the receiving end of military-technical transfers, since its own arms industry produces few highly sophisticated weapons systems. Therefore, China's ability to support and enhance Russian military enterprises is limited. For this reason, Russia is more keen on cooperation with Western arms-producing nations, such as France, which can provide two-way exchanges of ideas, models, and capital.

On the other hand, the thrust of China's defense policy will in the future point southeast, toward Taiwan and the South China Sea, rather than toward Russia and Central Asia. The entire South China Sea area, with its disputed archipelagos of Spratly, Paracel, and others, may be engaged in a long and intensive local arms race. Vietnam has already bought eight Russian SU-27 airplanes, and Malaysia made a significant purchase of MiG-29 fighters. Given this arms buildup, China will need Russian military technologies more than ever. Military orders already placed by Taiwan in the West and plans of further large-scale purchases guarantee that Beijing-Taipei enmity and the regional arms race will continue intensively for years to come.

The Taiwanese lag behind continental China in buying modern combat aircraft, but they are ready to spend more money, since they feel threatened. In 1992 Taipei signed agreements with France and the United States to procure sixty Mirage 2000-5 fighters (with an option for forty more) and 150 F-16s at a total cost of $10.8 billion. Taiwan has already received four E-2C Hawkeye early warning, command and control airplanes costing $700 million, while continental China has almost no electronic warfare systems.[9]

In response, Beijing signed a contract with Moscow in December 1995 for additional SU-27 fighters. The Chinese could bring the total number of those airplanes to fifty, which will give them the right to conclude a license contract for independent production of the SU-27 in order to modernize their air force—their long-standing intention.

The political situation in the world is fluid. In the mid-1990s, the West's attitude to both Beijing and Moscow has worsened due to several factors, such as the war in Chechnya and the situation between China and Taiwan. Facing NATO expansion to the East, Russia finds itself dangerously isolated, without any clear friends except Belarus. Many presume that the costs of Russian transfers of non-critical military and nuclear technologies to China and other stable Asian countries would be worth it to get out of geopolitical isolation.

All that really restrains any further movement to partnership with China is a myth of demographic expansion, the image of tens of millions of Chinese who are ready (or have already begun) to occupy "empty" Siberia. Controlling Chinese "tourist-traders" does not constitute a political problem, but rather one of law enforcement. Moreover, the Chinese authorities do not interfere with the punishment and extradition of visa violators. Central China is clearly overpopulated, yet the border areas of northern Manchuria have almost the same low population density as adjacent Russian territory. There is no "demographic edge." Cold Siberia and the Far East are not the most attractive areas for potential economic emigres, especially those from Central and Southern China. Furthermore, most Chinese dream of resettling in America, not Russia.

Mass migration to the northwest is possible in the event of an internal catastrophe, such as severe economic crisis combined with political destabilization. Therefore, Russia needs a strong and stable China, which will be able to guarantee steady bilateral relations and tranquility along the border.

Despite all internal and external attempts to impose the idea of a Chinese threat on Russian public opinion, no such menace exists. It should be noted that a rapprochement between Russia and China—to say nothing of a closer bilateral strategic partnership evolving into a military-political alliance—contradicts U.S. global policy aims. The dangerous nature of further rapprochement between Russia, China, and Iran was explicitly voiced by former CIA Director John Deutsch.

The process of realizing Russian national interests intensifies the desire to transform the purely commercial nature of today's military-technical cooperation with China into a basis for long-term strategic partnership and a new balance of power in Asia favorable to Russia. A strategic partnership with a group of the largest and most influential countries of continental Asia (China, Iran, and India) based on common interests and arms trade can help Russia stabilize the situation in Central Asia and secure its vulnerable southern borders. Such an arrangement will also help to restrain radical Islamic fundamentalism with non-violent methods and stave off what Moscow views as destabilizing Western and Turkish penetration into Central Asia and the Caspian basin.

Notes

[1]*The Military Balance 1994/95*. London: International Institute for Strategic Studies, 1994, 170-73.

[2]*SIPRI Yearbook 1995*, 333.

[3]*Asia 1994 Yearbook*. Hong Kong: Review Publishing Company, Hong Kong, 1994.

[4]Gill Bates and Teaho Kim. *China's Arms Acquisitions from Abroad: A Quest for 'Superb and Secret Weapons.'* Oxford: Oxford University Press, 1995, 49-50.

[5]Ibid, 138.

[6]*South China Morning Post*, March 19, 1993.

[7]*Jane's Defence Weekly*, November 19, 1994.

[8]Bureaucratic struggle can bring about absolutely improbable results. Thus, in the middle of 1994 a contract on the delivery of C-300 PMU-1 to China was signed, but no relevant governmental decision was ready at that moment! Only a true Russian bureaucrat who is well aware of all the subtleties of military-technical cooperation can fully realize the extraordinariness of the matter.

[9]*SIPRI Yearbook 1995*, 544-45.

Chapter 7

Russia, the Wassenaar Arrangement, and the Creation of International Restraints on Arms Transfers

Pyotr G. Litavrin

On December 19, 1995, an agreement reached in Wassenaar, Netherlands, established a new regime for controlling exports of conventional arms and dual-use technologies. In July 1996, the Wassenaar Arrangement on Export Controls for Conventional Arms and Dual-Use Goods and Technologies went into force. A total of thirty-three countries—including Russia, Ukraine, Poland, Hungary, the Czech Republic, and Slovakia—agreed to adhere to certain principles in their national arms-transfer policies, and to this end, compiled lists of sensitive weapons and technologies. After the text was reviewed by the Preparatory Committee, each member-state national government had to approve the provisions of the Wassenaar Arrangement. This new export control regime would formally terminate Cold War practices—started with the establishment of the Coordinating Committee for Multilateral Export Controls (COCOM) in 1949—of effectively "blacklisting" the Soviet Union from Western deliveries of arms and sophisticated technologies.

The road from COCOM to Wassenaar was neither short nor easy. Despite the resulting changes in political realities, neither the dissolution of the Warsaw Pact nor the disintegration of the Soviet Union in 1991 automatically led to the end of COCOM or a radical restructuring of the organization. It also could not be ignored that COCOM's prime target, Russia, was no longer the arch-enemy.

Thus COCOM became anachronistic, and in 1993 a number of states decided to create the Forum on Problems of Cooperation in the Field of Export Control over Modern Technologies, which was open for membership to the states of the former Soviet Union and its former satellites. The notion of not simply dissolving COCOM, but replacing it with an entirely new system to regulate arms exports and dual-use technologies stemmed from the fact that rogue states, not the U.S.S.R. or its former allies, principally concerned the West, led by the United States. Thus, the creation of such a "New Forum"[1] implied increased export restrictions on sales to so-called "rogue states" such as Iraq, Iran, North Korea, and Libya. Moreover, given the post–Cold War rise in instability that posed a potential threat to Western interests, it was increasingly felt that export controls over the transfer of sensitive items needed to focus on the Third World.

Notably, despite the liberalization of export controls for sales to Eastern Europe and the Baltic states, constraints on technology transfers and arms sales to Russia remained in force. Russia protested against continued restrictions, in particular those on generic dual-use items such as metalworking lathes, personal computers, and telecommunications facilities. These goods are hardly strategic or critical for developing Russia's defense industry. Many member-states criticized maintaining these restrictions, particularly the Europeans, who were keen on developing trade with Russia. Some skeptics claimed that American "caution" was actually stimulated by an unwillingness to provide Russia with modern technologies based on purely commercial considerations. Under such circumstances, Russia could not agree to join the forum.

Iraq's invasion of Kuwait, the development of missile and chemical warfare capabilities in Iraq, and missile development in North Korea, India, and Pakistan all stimulated concern within the Clinton administration. A growing number of experts in the Pentagon and State Department held that the main threat to U.S. interests no longer emanated from Moscow, but from the uncontrolled proliferation of weapons of mass destruction, including certain conventional armaments (e.g., missiles, advanced fighter-aircraft). It became all too obvious that, without Russia's close cooperation, an efficient system of export control to developing countries could not emerge. Thus

Washington revived the process of engaging Russia in arms control forums such as the Missile Technology Control Regime (MTCR) and what later became known as the Wassenaar Arrangement.

One of the most critical issues in Wassenaar's birth included the timeframe, terms, and conditions of Russia's eventual participation. On these questions, the West was divided from the very beginning. While the United States, Canada, and to a certain extent the United Kingdom attempted to delay Russia's admission, most Western European nations did not insist on any special conditions. Those favoring delay sought to gain additional political concessions from Moscow, such as terminating Russian military-technical cooperation with Iran. They also felt a need to secure a more efficient national system of export control in the Russian Federation. The other group, while it agreed to proceed cautiously and incrementally when removing trade restrictions with Russia, insisted on Moscow's prompt involvement in the process of establishing a post-COCOM organization. Discord and lack of cohesion among COCOM's members, did not, however, preclude their ultimate decision to formally dissolve the organization on March 31, 1994. Immediately, work commenced on establishing a new organization to exercise control over arms exports and dual-use goods and technologies. Initially, Russia was to be a founding member but, ironically, Russia only managed to join the process in its final stages a year and a half later.

* * *

After COCOM's dissolution, Washington quickly put forth its position that Moscow's arms sales and nuclear cooperation with Iran represented the principal obstacle to its involvement in the establishment of the New Forum. Why did that particular issue become so pivotal? Was the Clinton administration genuinely concerned about the growth of Iran's military capabilities, or did it provide a pretext to stall negotiations in order to wait and see which way the bitter domestic political crisis in Russia, which came to a head in 1993, would be resolved?

There are no simple answers. First, Russian-Iranian military cooperation obviously concerned the Clinton administration, whose negative attitude toward the present Iranian regime

107

is a matter of principle. Along with Iraq, Iran has become one of Washington's top adversaries in the region, subject to a policy of containment. President Clinton was also obliged to take into account U.S. domestic politics, namely the congressional resolve to impose sanctions against Russia if its cooperation (in particular, nuclear infrastructure transfers) with Iran continued. It mattered little to American leaders that the true extent of Russian-Iranian military-technical cooperation was limited. Russian deliveries did not include massive sales of destabilizing weapons such as missiles and bombers. Such a relationship is dwarfed in comparison with U.S. arms supplies to neighboring Saudi Arabia.

The "Iranian factor" was not the only obstacle to Russian involvement in the New Forum negotiations. Even after the adoption of a new Constitution in December 1993, domestic political instability in Russia, coupled with the growing influence of the Communist opposition, compelled Washington to proceed with caution. Russia's attempts to restore its former position in the world arms market and to penetrate the lucrative markets of Southeast Asia and the Persian Gulf indicated that it could not be discounted as a competitor to the United States.

The central reason for America's cautious approach was its lack of confidence in Russia's national export control system. The tightness of the export control system per se was not so much in question, for Russia's system generally complied with international standards. More dubious was Russia's ability to supervise cross-border deliveries, especially those to ex-Soviet republics. As noted in the *SIPRI Yearbook, 1995*, "these countries have not established effective systems for export regulation. Under these conditions, ending COCOM restrictions on Russia was, it was argued, premature."[2] Incidences of smuggling of nuclear fission materials, arms, and technologies from Russia and the bureaucratic chaos of 1993-94 buttressed these reservations. This was all reflected in the Clinton administration's official policy, which hinged Russia's membership in the future arrangement on a more stable domestic situation and its development of a national arms export control system that could conform to the New Forum's minimum requirements.

American hesitations were criticized sharply both in Washington and among the former COCOM member-states.

Critics charged that keeping Russia on the waiting list for too long could be counterproductive. In the United States, critics believed that such action would further strain Russian-American relations and undercut those in Russia who favored close cooperation with the West. Moreover, the United States gambled losing all leverage power over Russian export policy. The Clinton administration had to make a choice. The process of creating a New Forum was already under way, and the risk of Russia's absence could render the organization a futile verbal exercise.

As far as Russia itself was concerned, its quest for membership in international export control organizations like MTCR and the New Forum was spurred by its desire to penetrate international and particularly Western markets for arms and technologies, establish closer cooperation with industrialized nations, and, most important, abolish discriminatory COCOM restrictions. Politically, Russia's significant step to join such regimes helped eliminate remnants of Cold War foreign policy, establishing practical, not just verbal, cooperation with the West.

To achieve this, Russia in 1994-95 made a number of gestures to assuage U.S. concerns. During his fall 1994 visit to New York, President Yeltsin pledged not to conclude any new arms agreements with Iran, although previously signed contracts were to be honored. Welcoming that move, President Clinton immediately stressed at a White House press conference that Russia's inclusion in the New Forum talks largely depended on an evaluation of the scale and specifics of Russian commitments to Iran.

In any case, lingering doubts about the terms and conditions of Russia's involvement prevented it from participation in the first rounds of the New Forum talks held in September 1994 at The Hague and in February 1995 in Canberra, Australia. Only after the Yeltsin-Clinton summit in May 1995 in Moscow did a State Department spokesman acknowledge that Russian contracts would not endow Iran with any significant new capabilities, nor change the balance of power in the region. Thus, Russia's participation in the New Forum was cleared at last. The final agreement was reached at the meeting of U.S. Vice President Albert Gore and Russian Premier Viktor Chernomyrdin in Moscow on June 28-29, 1995.

After its concessions on military-technical cooperation with Iran, Russia expected not only full participation in the preparatory process but also the right to safeguard its legitimate national interests. This proved difficult, however, especially if one takes into account time constraints; the establishment of the New Forum was to be concluded in just a few months (i.e., before the end of 1995). While there was some indication that many Western nations desired to continue working into the first half of 1996, given the accession of Russia and the Central European nations, the original deadline was not revised, and the working groups hastily concluded their activities before the end of 1995.

* * *

An analysis of the documents and the statements made at the New Forum talks shows that the arrangement as codified in mid-1996 was quite different from the way it was conceived only a year earlier. Apart from establishing operational methods and mechanisms, the founding members were charged with the important task of delimiting the ratio of the regime's primary focus between arms sales and dual-use technologies. Initially, the American view was that "the new regime should give first priority to conventional arms and second priority to dual-use goods."[3] The United States garnered political support from Japan, which proposed the establishment of an International Organization on Preventing Arms Proliferation. Others suggested the creation of two distinct regimes, one solely for the control of armaments and another for dual-use technologies. Their purpose was clear: Dangers are posed by both arms deliveries and technology transfers to regions of existing or potential conflict.

Such "hot spots" were pinpointed in two geographical areas, the Middle East and South Asia, and in four individual "rogue states"—Iran, Iraq, Libya, and North Korea—where all arms deliveries were to be forbidden. Japan's position was understandable since it is prohibited from exporting arms by the Japanese Constitution. As for the United States, the new international agreements on conventional arms control were in line with its position to develop greater transparency and responsibility in the sphere of arms exports, like the adoption of the London Principles for Conventional Arms Sales and the creation of the U.N. Register of Conventional Arms. Furthermore, the forum was aimed at strengthening the dominant position of the United States in the world arms market. After all, the four outcast "rogue states" were large-scale buyers of Soviet and

Russian military equipment and could become Russia's clients in the future. As for South Asia, after a pause in the early 1990s, Moscow resumed military-technical cooperation with India.

The new regime's emphasis on arms sales as the main object of control, at the expense of exports of dual-use technologies, could hardly be met with enthusiasm by America's major export competitors, including France, Germany, and of course Russia. The Wassenaar Arrangement (unlike MTCR) is a regime that features transparency rather than imposes bans (that is, member-states are to impose strict national controls over exported items and to inform the partners on a group or individual basis of transfers of such items). Despite this fact, some participants regarded American proposals on advance notification and exchange of detailed information as unacceptable. Discussions on developing a regional orientation and the proposal to "blacklist" certain countries likewise came to naught. Nonetheless, this does not suggest that member-states can quietly deliver risky weapons to unstable regions. Mutual understanding on where it is now impossible to transfer arms and sensitive technologies has finally been reached: In the case of Iraq and Libya, international sanctions continue, and Iran is mistrusted by all, including Russia.

Finally, the failure to impose full-scale control over arms transfers was to a large extent the result of deep divisions among the founding members. Wassenaar embraced leading arms exporters as well as a number of industrialized nations ranking among the major importers of weapons. That the large exporters organized themselves as the "big five," and later as the "big six,"[4] was not always approved of by the importers. The arms exporting countries, however, pointed to their special interests, which they refused to discuss with the others.

In any case, the desirability, in the eyes of the United States and other Western nations, of having an active small group within the new arrangement indicates that Wassenaar is yet to become a comprehensive and efficient arms export control regime. Similar ideas of transparency —*post factum* information exchanges on arms supplies and advance notification of deliveries, including a more specific indication of weapon type and model—were first advanced in dialogue over the U.N. Register of Conventional Arms in 1992 and 1994.

Despite good intentions, new regimes (MTCR, the Australia group, and the Wassenaar Arrangement) discriminate against non-members. Membership in such regimes should be made more attractive to non-members, notably China. The regimes can work to promote responsible and civilized behavior in the world arena and encourage unilateral restraint by demonstrating that such restrictions meet the interests of the respective state as well as enhance international security. The successful development and implementation of the Wassenaar Arrangement can promote genuine equality and partnership among member-states, furnishing a role model for non-members.

So far, equal partnership among member-states in Wassenaar is far from ideal. Russia is reported to remain on the technology-transfer restricted-country lists of a number of founding members, including the United States. This not only runs contrary to the spirit of partnership but is a clear act of discrimination. Russia also appears in new U.S. trade-restriction lists, such as the computer export regulations adopted in October 1995. Before Russia's membership in Wassenaar, such cases could be justified by bureaucratic inertia or hesitations about Russian compliance with regime requirements. At this juncture, however, no reasonable explanation can be offered.

Russia is also constrained by its need to understand what was already agreed upon before it joined the organization. As noted, in three months, Russia needed to cover the same ground that others covered in a year and a half. Preparatory work held behind closed doors was characterized by bitter struggles in defense of national positions. France, Switzerland, and Japan were not ready to abandon key interests for the sake of consensus. The final stages of inaugurating the Wassenaar Arrangement were thus difficult and intense, as exemplified by the fact that the initial concept of the agreement and its final version diverged, implementation was postponed, and a special Preparatory Committee had to be established to coordinate national positions.

As a result of closer cooperation between Russia and the West, a discriminatory position toward and constraints on Russia will gradually be eliminated. However, Russia's experience with negotiations for the Wassenaar Arrangement was unfavorable.

First of all, Russia did not understand the rush to complete the agreement by the end of 1995. Moreover, the United States failed to keep its promise to remove Russia from national trade restriction lists. In any case, joining Wassenaar at the final stage was a blow to Russia's international prestige.

It is important to note the overall context of Russia's last-minute admission to the new export control arrangement. NATO enlargement, U.S. attempts to push Russia out of its traditional East European arms markets, and political steps aimed at preventing Russian arms exports to the Asia-Pacific region and the Gulf states show that mutual understanding in this sphere is yet to be seen. The United States has a right to protect its own interests in the field of arms exports and technology transfers; but Russia, given the unequal state of the partnership, must be wary of conditions and restrictions set on its participation in international organizations.

Russia's admission also poses a number of other issues, such as the participation of Belarus and Kazakhstan (currently not members of Wassenaar), with which Russia forms a Customs Union. Furthermore, a complete cessation of Russian military-technical cooperation with Iran still remains to be demonstrated. While these problems are secondary to the ultimate goals of the export control regime, their underestimation could undermine Russia's credibility as a reliable partner.

Even without the "Russian factor," Wassenaar has not yet developed into a balanced international export control regime. For political reasons, a consensus was hastened. National export control systems were diverging to such an extent that coming to any agreement on an efficient export control regime became increasingly arduous. Former U.S. Under Secretary of State Lynn Davis confirmed the difficulties of bridging the gap between American and European approaches to Wassenaar. Press articles called for speedy action for another reason: the national elections in both the United States and Russia.

As a result of these factors, Wassenaar is a regime that is rather incomplete. Its final declaration has only limited practical meaning and is not binding. The arms control component is weak. Moreover, it does not meet U.S. expectations as an instrument to monitor arms flows and, more important, arms manufacturing technologies.

It may, however, be premature to pass final judgment on the nature, direction, and principles of the post-COCOM organization. Much can still be done to make the Arrangement a truly effective instrument for export control. In conclusion, it should be recognized that Russian participation in the Wassenaar Arrangement represents a major development, both for Russian politics and for international arms control efforts.

Notes

[1] What eventually became the Wassenaar Arrangement process was originally dubbed the "Post-COCOM Meetings" and subsequently the "New Forum."

[2] *SIPRI Yearbook 1995*, 620.

[3] *United States Information Agency News Bulletin*. U.S. Embassy, Moscow, May 18, 1995, 1.

[4] Italy became an addition to the original small group of France, Germany, Russia, the United Kingdom, and the United States.

Chapter 8

Arms Trade Rivalry in the Future of Russian-American Relations

Dmitri V. Trenin with Andrew J. Pierre

The arms trade could easily become a source of major tensions in Russian-American relations. Ironically, during the Cold War, arms sales rivalry was limited because both the United States and Russia restricted transfers to their own allies and friends. Thus the arms trade functioned as a separate, generally conflict-free area of relations between the superpowers. In today's more fluid world, however, new complexities and contradictions have emerged that could lead to far more serious confrontation than has ever existed before.

When the bipolar system of international relations prevailed, each of the two competing superpowers supplied arms and military technology to its own allies and clients. Strategic considerations dominated arms-export policy in both Moscow and Washington. The handful of nations that benefited from concurrent Soviet and American arms deliveries—for example, Finland, Yugoslavia, and India—usually used arms supply relationships to sustain not only military-technical diversification but also political balance. While Soviet-American rivalry extended to all corners of the globe, each superpower generally observed distinct zones of influence. At the same time, each "camp" constituted a market in itself. Thus weapons proliferation did not cause excessive friction in bilateral relations between the U.S.S.R. and the United States.

This situation has changed drastically with the end of the Cold War. Clear-cut spheres of influence have become less distinct as the arms market has become more globalized. At the same time, the market has shrunk, and Russian and American

115

arms traders now compete in the same national and regional markets. The very nature of relations between Moscow and Washington has changed. Confrontation and rivalry have dwindled with U.S. ascension as the dominant power.

Nevertheless, the long-term nature of Russian-American relations in this domain remains highly uncertain. In 1991-92, it seemed that Russia would assume the role of Washington's younger and loyal partner, but starting in 1993, Moscow's foreign policy began to articulate its national interest differences. In this context, the question of Russian arms deliveries to countries deemed "inappropriate" by American standards emerged for the first time. This was followed, to a lesser extent, by concern over potential U.S. arms supplies to former Warsaw Pact members or to the Newly Independent States (NIS) of the former Soviet Union. By the mid-1990s, the arms trade had became one of the sources of irritation in Russian-American relations. The reasons are multiple and range from perceptions resulting from differing psychological reactions, to commercial considerations, to domestic development in both countries.

Psychological Perceptions and Myth-Building

Democratic intellectuals in the Soviet Union considered arms exports to be "immoral." However, this notion quickly waned in Russian public opinion (similarly to the failed attempt by American liberals in the inter-war period of 1920-30 to change the nation's attitude toward the "death trade"). The abrupt deterioration in arms sales brought about a political and psychological shift in the opposite direction. During the Soviet era, information on military and technological cooperation with foreign countries was covered with a thick veil of secrecy. It is only natural that the absence of reliable data was compensated for by rumors and hearsay. When the first glimpses of accurate information on Soviet arms exports appeared in the late 1980s in accordance with the policy of glasnost, the subject immediately became a garden for myth creation.

One of the most widespread ideas in Russia in the early 1990s was that America was trying to push Russia out of the world arms market, including areas traditionally controlled exclusively by the U.S.S.R.[1] Aggressive arms trade competition was regarded as a quintessential example of U.S. exploitation of Russia's weak position. Military-political circles in Russia believed that the true aim of U.S. policy was to cripple the Russian military-industrial complex. Defense manufacturing and services do not comprise as limited a portion of the national economy in Russia as they do in the United States; they encompass most of Russia's high-technology sector. Therefore, in the opinion of many Russians, the United States, while providing limited assistance for reforms, designed to secure zero competition from a post-Communist Russia.

This notion was supported by U.S. Congressional Research Service data on the comparative volume of arms and military equipment exports. From 1990 to 1994, the United States made half of all arms agreements with the Third World, with its share rising to 74 percent in 1993, when Russia's share amounted to less than 10 percent.[2] This 7-to-1 ratio is particularly striking if one takes into account the fact that, as recently as 1987, the ratio was almost even. Soviet exports had even topped American exports to the Third World during several years in the 1980s.

At first glance, these figures speak for themselves. Yet they must be placed in a broader context to be correctly understood. First, there has been overall shrinkage in the global arms market, and American arms transfers have not expanded in real terms. They remain more or less the same (at annual levels of about $10 billion), whereas Russian arms exports had virtually collapsed by 1992 (some sources indicate a fall from $27 billion in 1987 to a low point of $1.7 billion in 1994). Second, the collapse of Russian arms exports was not caused by an American takeover of traditional Soviet markets, but by geopolitical and geostrategic shifts that virtually eliminated the system of Soviet alliances and allegiances. In none of the former Warsaw Pact countries or "socialist orientation" nations ranging from Angola to Afghanistan has the United States replaced Russia as the major arms supplier. Third, political instability and bureaucratic chaos in Russia, especially in 1992-93, as well as an acute, decade-long economic crisis undermined arms importers' confidence in their Russian partners; during this period, many traditional purchasers of Russian weapons suffered from irregular

117

supplies of spare parts and other inconveniences. Finally, in the early 1990s, the United Nations imposed an arms embargo on a number of traditional customers of Soviet materiel—namely, Iraq, Libya, and the republics of former Yugoslavia.

On the other hand, it should be noted that revenues from Russian arms exports did not fall as dramatically as did the actual deliveries of equipment. The U.S.S.R. often delivered arms on very beneficial conditions, with low interest repayment schemes extending to fifteen to twenty years and sometimes even thirty to forty years. A significant part of the $90 billion debt owed to Moscow by a number of Asian, African, and Latin American nations stems from overly generous arms credits, and repayment of even a small portion of that money is seen as highly problematic.[3]

Moreover, in the post–Cold War environment, Russian arms suppliers have the opportunity to penetrate markets that were in the past completely controlled by the West. Unlike the majority of erstwhile Soviet clients, many of these countries—notably those in the Persian Gulf and Southeast Asia—have significant financial resources. Russian arms dealers' persistence in cracking these markets has already achieved results, despite fierce competition with the United States and a number of other countries.

Unexpected help also came from Germany. In an attempt to get rid of surplus arms inherited from the East German National People's Army, Germany passed on Soviet-built arms to NATO allies Greece and Turkey. In addition, the Bundeswehr accepted Soviet MiG-29 fighters. As a result, new markets were suddenly created for spare parts and future upgrades. The U.S. government did not impede any of these processes.

Stabilization of Russian arms sales followed a period of sharp decline and very slow growth in the mid-1990s. The myth that America desired to drive Russia out of the market is gradually subsiding, but the imagined problems are giving way to real ones.

A Conflict of Commercial Interests

Unlike the previous two decades, the global arms trade of the 1990s is dominated by commercial rather than strategic competition. Now that diplomatic rivalry has been reduced and an ideological struggle has become a relic of the past, economic pressures are more apparent. These were emphasized by defense industries in practically all of the leading world powers that faced a crisis when the so-called "peace dividend" reduced arms production.

A sharp fall in government orders made manufacturers in Russia and the United States seek a solution in exports. The crisis in which the military-industrial complexes of the two countries found themselves was similar, despite the enormous difference in severity. In 1992, Russian government orders virtually terminated. Yet Russia's military-industrial complex is much more important for its national economy than the American defense industry is for the U.S. economy. Moreover, conversion of Russia's huge defense industry is slow, subject to a painful transition from a communist administrative economy to a market-oriented one. In the United States, reductions, no matter how painful, are proceeding far more smoothly because of the general flexibility of corporate structures and the mobility of American labor. Russians frequently have to fight for the physical survival of not only individual enterprises but also whole branches of industry and technology. Export strategy is one instrument of that struggle. According to one well-placed official, in the mid-1990s, about 400,000 jobs in the Russian defense industry depend on export orders.[4]

The mission to "recapture abandoned positions" in export markets was put forward by President Boris Yeltsin.[5] The Clinton administration, in turn, lifted many self-imposed restrictions on arms exports. Thus, Russian-American competition in the arms trade has a real foundation, and the growing need to export arms in the shrinking world arms market renders that competition ever more fierce and acute. The first half of the 1990s demonstrated some examples of this competition that we consider illustrative.

India

In 1992, U.S. pressure forced Russia to cancel a sale of cryogenic rocket motor technology to India. Moscow confined itself to deliveries of motors without the sensitive technology. Russian government officials did not share American suspicions over India's intentions and capabilities with respect to missile tech-

119

nology, and Russia made several attempts to resist U.S. pressure. However, the technology part of the deal was finally cancelled.

This event left a bad taste in the mouth of the Russians, because of the public humiliation of succumbing to U.S. pressure and the missed profit (which was partially compensated by new Russian-American contracts on space cooperation). Furthermore, Moscow lost prestige in the eyes of India, which has been a traditional strategic partner. Suspicions arose that the true motive of U.S. pressure was not strategic concern but an attempt to "strangle" the Russian missile and space industry. The American triumph in the dispute promoted the belief in Russia that the United States is always after its own economic benefits.

Iran

Iran is one of the most vivid examples of Russian-American conflict in the arms trade realm. The United States officially accused Teheran of international terrorism and regarded Russian-Iranian military-technical cooperation as irresponsible opportunism. Russia, in turn, claimed that Washington's reaction was overly emotional and ideologically motivated. For its part, Moscow tends to balance Iran as a counterweight to Turkish influence in Central Asia and Transcaucasia. Tensions over Iran tightened in 1994-95 and have demonstrated the increased capability of Russian arms manufacturers to act on their own interests. Unlike the cancelled delivery of missile technology to India, the Russian military-industrial complex is not prepared to retreat on Iran. They may very well flout President Yeltsin's 1995 promises to the United States not to undertake new arms sales to Teheran beyond existing contracts. According to some sources, Russia would earn about $1 billion a year with the realization of some potential weapons sales. Although conventional arms manufacturers cannot rely on an agency with the same weight as MINATOM (the Ministry of Atomic Industry), Russian arms exporters are confident of finding better understanding in governmental quarters, given changes in the domestic political situation.

The U.S. policy of containment and isolation of Iran has left Teheran no choice other than to improve relations with Russia and China. Russian political circles point out that, after

Moscow's refusal (under U.S. pressure) to deliver a gas centrifuge to Iran, Teheran developed a new deal with China. American ambivalence to the Iranian-Chinese agreement convinced Moscow that "it is bad to be weak."

China

The subject of Russian arms deliveries to China is not formally on the agenda of Russian-American relations, but it is likely to be there in the future. Russian arms exports to China have yet to reach the amount and technological level to induce serious U.S. anxiety, but as Russian sales continue, Washington's concern is rising. While China's development as a military superpower is years away, Russia's role in this process may prove significant. China's use of Russian weapons in the Taiwan straits or the South China Sea would create serious problems for Russian-American relations.

Central and Eastern Europe

For Russia, the probability of losing arms markets in the former Warsaw Pact countries is alarming, though not as alarming as NATO expansion, the main point of contention between Moscow and the West. Nevertheless, the loss of those traditional markets is already considered to be a significant economic setback. Russia is especially concerned about U.S. proposals to sell fighter planes to Poland and Hungary as a way of enhancing the Partnership for Peace Program. The Pentagon is strongly supporting arms deals with states in Central and Eastern Europe. Russian officials assume that the United States will use these sales to achieve a set of strategic goals: expanding the market for U.S. military goods, modernizing Central European forces to meet Western standards, and promoting inter-operability with NATO forces. Another U.S. goal, in the opinion of many Russians, is to cause additional damage to Russia's military-industrial complex.

Potential Conflicts

Today, importing states have an unprecedented choice of suppliers for armaments. Their choice depends largely on factors such as the level of technological sophistication, price, and terms of acquisition. The international and political influence of

121

the exporting country is key as well. Military-technical cooperation is considered as a factor that could to a certain extent guarantee a customer's security. On all of these counts, Russia and America stand on vastly different ground. The victory of the U.S.-led coalition in Desert Storm against Iraq not only boosted the prestige of American weapons but also the value of American security guarantees. In contrast, Russia's attempts to suppress insurgency in Chechnya only demonstrated the degree of Russia's military degradation and raised serious doubts about the quality of Russian arms on the battlefield.[6]

Russia's traditional advantage in arms sales has been low prices, often set arbitrarily low for strategic reasons. But this advantage has quickly faded. Now, the cost of power, raw materials, and labor must be accounted for in setting the price. Economic competitiveness in production now constitutes a major element for Russia's success in the arms trade.

America's relative strength vis-à-vis Russia has consolidated the belief that the United States is a natural adversary of Russia's military-industrial complex.[7] Although this may pale in comparison to the heyday of the Cold War, economic interest could play a role in recreating strategic competition between Moscow and Washington in certain regions. Along with China, the United States has been accused of "intellectual piracy."[8] U.S. arms traders are accused of "dishonorable trade practices," and the U.S. government is blamed for "political pressure."[9]

Even some comparatively moderate circles in the Russian establishment fear that aggressive American promotion of arms on the world market would leave the Russian military-industrial complex with the limited (and unfavorable) choice of exporting either to "rogue" states or to former Soviet clients. According to that logic, the United States indirectly forces Russia to export to Iran and China, which in turn have limited choices as well. In the future, the number of Russian arms customers could include Libya and Iraq, which during the Soviet era constituted about 20 percent of the U.S.S.R.'s total arms sales revenues.[10] In 1995, Russia actively began preparations for restoring economic relations with these countries in the expectation of a time when U.N. sanctions will be lifted (an action Moscow has consistently promoted). At an international conference on Political Problems of Export Control held in Moscow in April 1994, it was stressed that "traditional importers of Russian arms and technologies are the states that can too easily be accused of actions aimed to disrupt international security."[11] Cuba and Syria are two other examples of traditional importers of Russian weapons who might again be purchasers—although they have limited financial resources to pay for Russian arms.

Some U.S. actions have caused strong reactions in Russia. In 1994-95, Russia criticized the U.S. Congress's position on removing the arms embargo of the Moslem government of Bosnia-Herzegovina. After the Dayton-Paris peace agreements, Russia refused to take part in the Istanbul conference devoted to a renewal of arms deliveries to Bosnian Moslems. Some of Moscow's opposition to NATO expansion stems from its fear of losing former Warsaw Pact arms markets. Furthermore, any hypothetical consideration of supplying U.S. arms to the Baltic states provokes harsh reactions in Moscow. Russian military-political circles even displayed dismay at single-item deliveries by the United States of samples to CIS countries (e.g., military patrol boats for Kazakhstan).

In this vein, one should recall the difficulties of establishing a new structure to replace COCOM. The United States agreed to Russian participation only six months before the conclusion of the Wassenaar Arrangement in December 1995. The Arrangement came into force in July 1996, much later than originally planned, because of differences between Russia and the United States. Although it deals with arms on a global level, the Wassenaar Arrangement will impose restrictions on exports to Iran, Iraq, Libya, and North Korea—all of which are traditional customers of Russian defense equipment.

It may happen that Russian and American weapons will again be accumulated on different sides of the front-line, as in the Cold War or Desert Storm. One real danger of the Bosnian conflict was the possibility that all arms embargoes would be lifted, resulting in massive American arms supplies to Moslems and Croatians and Russian arms supplies to Serbs. In the course of military demonstrations off the shore of Taiwan in March 1996, to cite another example, Russian-built SU-27 fighters of the Chinese air force confronted F-5 airplanes of Taiwan.

Arms manufacturers have made their own conclusions: Be tough and, when necessary, ruthless.[12] Russian officials argue that their country has lived up to its international obligations for controlling weapons exports. They claim that the Russian export control system has been tightened to exclude arms supply to potential conflict zones and to unstable regimes. By 1995, a straightforward system of arms export control was established. The system is centered on the Russian President himself, who controls it both through his assistant on military-technical cooperation and through the Russian Security Council. Russian arms dealers became much more aggressive and gained marketing experience their Soviet predecessors lacked. As a result, Russian arms deliveries started a rise from the admittedly low base of $1.7 billion in 1994 to $3.2 billion in 1995 and to about $3.8 billion in 1996. The value of sales contracts signed by mid-1996 reached $7 billion and was still rising.[13] Russia even overtook the United States in terms of arms sales agreements to the developing world in 1995.[14]

Thus the Russian arms industry is gradually strengthening its ability to export and reclaiming its past position. This promises further growth of competition in the world market, where Russia can in time become a major competitor of the United States.

Dangers of Commercial Competition and Prospects for Regulating Rivalry

The commercialization of the arms trade is not a phenomenon to be ambivalent about. Countries may now possess advanced military technologies never before in their inventories. This could change the strategic landscape drastically. Even now regional arms races are being fueled that are scarcely controlled from the outside. The "discipline" of bipolar Cold War confrontation is evaporating. Presumably friendly nations are being pumped up with armaments regardless of the consequences for internal political upheaval or regional destabilization.

For example, the United States and Russia are competing to sell the most modern weapons to those rising Asian nations that feel they cannot rely on purely economic instruments to protect their national interests. Having forgotten about the fate of huge arsenals sold to the Shah of Iran in the 1970s, the United States continues to deliver large quantities of arms to

King Fahd of Saudi Arabia. Russia delivers weapons to China, despite Russia's weakening position in the Far East and the clear growth in power of its great neighbor.

There are strong industrial forces in both countries that are reluctant to accept restraint as they try to survive in a world of shrinking demand for arms, both worldwide and domestic. No compromise, such as a division of markets or joint production and marketing, seems likely at the moment. Much like Cold War strategy, the contemporary arms trade is regarded as a zero-sum game. The United States, which is obviously on top today, is reluctant to cultivate a future competitor. Russia, which hoped to divide the market and advance joint production, is disillusioned.

It would be a mistake, however, to think that rivalry cannot be regulated in principle. Despite possible economic gains, national interests should not be reduced to maximizing arms sales. Both countries are interested in regional stability and non-proliferation of high-tech weapons that could make Russian and American armed forces more vulnerable. One should not forget the example of Iraq, which, having imported $58 billion worth of armaments, provoked a regional crisis that took even more money to defuse. It would also be useful to remember the Soviet experience of helping Germany create its air force and tank troops in the 1920s—or Soviet assistance to China in the 1950s for the development of nuclear weapons.

Russian-American competition is softened by the fact that after the end of the Cold War, Russia is not the only—and in many areas not the strongest—competitor of the United States. In principle, Russia falls into a category that also includes France and other West European nations. At the same time, the United States is not the only—and sometimes not the main—competitor of Russia, since arms dealers of Western and Central Europe, China, Israel, and Ukraine also try to get hold of former Soviet markets.

As a result, in purely commercial terms, Russian-American competition in the world market may not take extreme forms. There are hopes that it will be adjusted in a somewhat natural market-oriented manner. The Russians are gradually filling the former Soviet niche, with the Americans basically keeping their own dominant position in regions such as Latin America. A

125

number of countries, for instance those in the Persian Gulf, purchase Russian weapons to obtain unofficial guarantees of security; others, like Malaysia and its neighbors, seek to diversify the sources of their arms imports. "Invasions" of new markets cannot be massive or quick. Even those Central European nations that may soon join NATO will find the process of transition to Western arms and equipment long and costly. Poland, which is more interested in joining NATO than many of its neighbors, continues to buy MiG-29 airplanes from the Czech Republic and is considering limited military-technical cooperation with Russia.

Of course arms control is not just a bilateral Russian-American problem, but one requiring truly international cooperation. Thirty-three nations, including Russia, have now joined the Wassenaar Arrangement, whose purpose is to regulate transfers of conventional arms and "dual-use technologies." Russia can play an important role in the Wassenaar regime if it so desires. Arms export regulations can also be discussed at other international forums, such as the Organization for Security and Cooperation in Europe (OSCE), the West European Union (WEU), or the Commonwealth of Independent States (CIS). In such forums, one can more realistically expect the limitation of damage to common interests than the complete harmonization of the interests of all.

Conflicts of interest arising from arms trade competition between Russia and the United States could exert a deeply negative influence on the development of Russian-American relations as a whole. In the long-run, however, political relations are likely to take precedence over economic gains. In the most important arms transfer controversies likely to arise, political and strategic interests will continue to override those of commercial advantage. While complete harmony between Russia and the United States over the arms trade is an unlikely prospect, rivalry will hopefully be limited.

Notes

[1] A typical example can be seen in the following quotation: "Russia has reduced its arms sales and, immediately, other countries dramatically enlarged their arms production and quickly filled the vacuum. Today the United States controls over 50 percent of the world arms exports." See Vladimir Kosarev, "Russia Must Occupy Its Place in the Arms Market," *Krasnaya Zvezda*, January 6, 1994, 3.

[2] U.S. Library of Congress, Congressional Research Service. *Conventional Arms Transfers to the Developing Nations, 1987 - 1994*. Washington, 1995.

[3] Kazennov, Sergei. "Arms Trade and Arms Transfers Policy From Reform to Stabilisation: Russian Foreign, Military, and Economic Policy (Analysis and Forecast) 1993-1995." *Russian Industrial Review*. Moscow: Moscow State Institute of International Relations (MGIMO), 139.

[4] Nikolay V. Mikhailov, Deputy Secretary of the Russian Security Council, speaking at a seminar at Carnegie Moscow Center on September 5, 1995.

[5] *Rossiyskaya Gazeta*, November 18, 1993.

[6] See, for instance, publications in Moskovsky Komsomolets in January-February 1995.

[7] Noteworthy in this connection is the utterance of Air Marshal Yevgeny Shaposhnikov, the President's representative in *Rosvooruzheniye*, who remarked that "the end of the Cold War is more relative than real." *Izvestia*, April 12, 1994.

[8] Nikolai Zlenko, "Russian Weapons," *Krasnaya Zvezda*, February 25, 1995, 3.

[9] Sergei Oslikovsky, Deputy General Director of *Rosvooruzheniye*. Quoted in Segodnya, September 29, 1994, 1.

[10] Interview of Gen. Victor Samoilov, General Director of Rosvooruzheniye in *Nezavisimaya Gazeta*, April 28, 1994.

[11] Igor Korotchenko. "Bribes Can Well Be Resorted To," *Nezavisimaya Gazeta*, September 27, 1994.

[12] *Krasnaya Zvezda*, March 29, 1996, 1.

[13] *Finansoviye Izvestia*, No.36 (270), April 4, 1996, 11.

[14] U.S. Library of Congress, *Congressional Research Service. Conventional Arms Transfers to Developing Nations, 1988–1995*. Washington, 1996, 5.

Appendix

Russian-American Working Group on Conventional Arms Proliferation

Co-Chairmen:
Andrew J. Pierre, *Carnegie Endowment for International Peace*
Dmitri V. Trenin, *Moscow Center of the Carnegie Endowment*

Participants*:
Alexei G. Arbatov, *Deputy Chair, Defense Committee, the State Duma*
Leonid V. Astashkov, *State Committee for Defense Industries*
Vladimir P. Averchev, *Secretary, Foreign Relations Committee, the State Duma*
Norbert Baas, *Counselor, Embassy of Germany, Moscow*
Alexander N. Basov, *Rosvooruzheniye*
Sergei F. Belov, *Russian Institute of Strategic Studies*
Capt. Stanislav V. Beribulov, *Defense Attache, Embassy of Belarus, Moscow*
Sergei Blagovolin, *Director-General, ORT Television*
Ian Bond, *First Secretary, Embassy of the United Kingdom, Moscow*
Scott Bruckner, *Director, Carnegie Moscow Center (1995-1997)*
Sheila Buckley, *U.S. Department of Defense*
Richard Burger, *Director, Carnegie Moscow Center (1993-1995)*
William Burns, *Minister-Counselor for Political Affairs, Embassy of the United States, Moscow*
Christophe Carle, *Director of Research, French Institute of International Relations*
Christopher Cheang, *Charge d'affaires, Embassy of Singapore, Moscow*
Alexander A. Dynkin, *Deputy Director, Institute for World Economy and International Relations*
Yurii Efimov, *Ministry for Defense Industries*
Konstantin Eggert, *Diplomatic Correspondent*, Izvestia
Steven Erlanger, *Moscow Bureau Chief,* The New York Times
Pavel Felgengauer, *Defense Correspondent*, Segodnya
Yurii V. Fisun, *Rosvooruzheniye*
Lars Freden, *Minister-Counselor, Embassy of Sweden, Moscow*

* Participated in at least one meeting.

Col. Yurii N. Gaidukov, *Committee on Military-Technical Policy, Russian Ministry of Defense*

Sherman Garnett, *Senior Associate, Carnegie Endowment for International Peace*

Anatoli F. Gerasymov, *Senior Associate, National Institute for Strategic Studies, Ukraine*

Mikhail I. Gerasyov, *Deputy Director, Institute for the U.S.A. and Canada*

Michael Gfoeller, *First Secretary, Embassy of the United States, Moscow*

Bates Gill, *Project Leader, Stockholm International Peace Research Institute*

Francois Goldblatt, *Counselor, Embassy of France, Moscow*

Alexander M. Golts, *Political Observer,* Krasnaya Zvezda

Col. Sergei G. Gorbunov, *Military Staff, Commonwealth of Independent States*

Vladimir G. Greshnikov, *Chief Expert, Rosvooruzheniye*

Yurii P. Grishin, *Advisor to the Chairman, Committee on Military-Technical Policy, Russian Ministry of Defense*

Fred Hiatt, The Washington Post

Gints Jegermans, *Counselor, Embassy of Latvia, Moscow*

Ethan Kapstein, *Organization for Economic Co-operation and Development, Paris*

Sergei A. Karaganov, *Deputy Director, Institute of Europe; Member, Presidential Council*

Bilahari Kausikan, *Ambassador of Singapore, Moscow*

Gennadi K. Khromov, *Ministry for Defense Industries*

Viktor M. Khromov, *Russian Presidential Administration*

Vladimir P. Kireev, *President, Russian Academy of Rocketry and Artillery*

Irina Kobrinskaya, *Program Associate, Carnegie Moscow Center*

Stanislav N. Kondrashov, Izvestia

Alexander A. Konovalov, *President, Institute for Strategic Assessments*

Vladimir S. Korneevets, *Director, Information and Analysis Center, Russian Ministry of Defense*

Sergei V. Kortunov, *Deputy Chief of Staff, Russian National Security Council*

Maj. Gen. Alexander Kotelkin, *Director-General, Rosvooruzheniye*

Sergei A. Koulik, *Director, Center for Military-Strategic Studies*

Yevgeni M. Kozhokin, *Director, Russian Institute of Strategic Studies*

Vadim B. Kozyulin, *Center for Political Studies in Russia*

Andrei A. Kurasov, *Chief Expert, Promradteckbank*

Rustem S. Kurmanguzhin, *First Secretary, Embassy of Kazakhstan, Moscow*

Ellen Laipson, *Director, Middle Eastern and South Asian Affairs, U.S. National Security Council*

Brig. Gen. Gustav Lange, *Defense Attache, Embassy of Germany, Moscow*

Pyotr G. Litavrin, *Russian Ministry of Foreign Affairs*

John Lloyd, The Financial Times, *London*

Vadim V. Makarenko, *Deputy Editor-in-Chief,* Novoye Vremya

Gen. Mikhail D. Malei, *Chairman, Interagency Committee on Scientific and Technological Problems, Russian Security Council*

Robert B. Mantel, *Senior Advisor, Bureau on Political-Military Affairs, U.S. Department of State*

Gale Mattox, *U.S. Department of State*

Alexei P. Mayorov, *Soyuz Company*

Michael McFaul, *Senior Associate, Carnegie Endowment for International Peace*

Nikolai V. Mikhailov, *Deputy Secretary, Russian Security Council*

Maj. Gen. Viktor N. Mironov, *Acting Chair, Committee on Military-Technical Policy*

Leonid M. Mlechin, *Deputy Editor-in-Chief,* Izvestia

Vladimir S. Myasnikov, *Director, Russia-China Center, Institute of Far Eastern Studies*

Vitaly V. Naumkin, *President, Center of Strategic and International Studies*

Ambassador Yurii K. Nazarkin, *Institute of Structural and Investment Studies*

Col. Nikolai G. Nazaryuk, *Defense Attache, Embassy of Ukraine, Moscow*

Gennadi S. Nikitin, *State Institute for Aerosystems*

Mikhail V. Nuzhdinov, *Federal Security Service*

Vladimir A. Orlov, *Director, Center for Political Studies in Russia*

Andre Ouiellet, *Counselor, Embassy of Canada, Moscow*

Robert Owen-Jones, *First Secretary, Embassy of Australia, Moscow*

Sergei K. Oznobishchev, *Director, Institute for Strategic Assessments*

Vladimir A. Pakhomov, *Deputy Chairman, Committee on Military-Technical Policy, Russian Ministry of Defense*

Alexander A. Pappe, *Rosvooruzheniye*

Jean Patrikainen, *Defense Technology Attache, Embassy of France, Moscow*

Alexander A. Pikayev, *Program Associate, Carnegie Moscow Center*

Alexander A. Piskunov, *Deputy Chairman, Defense Committee, first State Duma*

Alexei K. Pushkov, *Director, Public Relations, ORT Television*

Sergei M. Rogov, *Director, Institute for the U.S.A. and Canada*

Eugene Rumer, *RAND Corporation*

Konstantin O. Sarkisov, *Director, Center for Japanese Studies*

Maj. Gen. Alexander M. Sazonov, *Federal Security Service*

Kori N. Schake, *U.S. Department of Defense*

Maj. Georgii N. Sergienko, *Assistant Defense Attache, Embassy of Ukraine, Moscow*

Steven Sestanovich, *Vice President, Carnegie Endowment for International Peace*

Igor Shalupov, *Federal Security Service*

Alexei N. Shulunov, *President, Defense Industrialists League*

Paul Stares, *Brookings Institution, Washington*

Col. Nikolai V. Streshnev, *Military Staff, Commonwealth of Independent States*

Col. Sook Ho Li, *Defense Attache, Embassy of the Republic of Korea, Moscow*

Sun Linqiang, *Second Secretary, Embassy of China, Moscow*

Viktor M. Surikov, *Director-General, Institute of Defense Studies*

Col. Nikolai B. Surkov, *Information and Analysis Center, Russian Ministry of Defense*

Igor I. Terekhov, *State Institute for Aerosystems*

Lt. Col. Timothy Thomas, *U.S. Army General Staff and Command College*

Ambassador Roland M. Timerbaev, *President, Center for Political Studies in Russia*

Mikhail L. Titarenko, *Director, Institute for Far Eastern Studies*

Col. Oleg A. Tsyganov, *Information and Analysis Center, Russian Ministry of Defense*

Mikhail S. Vinogradov, *Committee of Scientists for Global Security*

Masato Watanabe, *First Secretary, Embassy of Japan, Moscow*

Carola Weil, *Women in International Security, U.S.A.*

Yota Yamamoto, *First Secretary, Embassy of Japan, Moscow*

Stephen Young, *First Secretary, Embassy of the United States, Moscow*

Alexander M. Zherebin, *Deputy Director, State Institute for Aerosystems*

Anton Zhigulsky, Defense News, The Moscow Times

Vladimir N. Zhuravliov, *Moscow Aviation Institute*

Andrei I. Zobov, *Program Associate, Carnegie Moscow Center*

Maj. Gen. Pavel S. Zolotaryov, *Director, Information and Analysis Center, Russian Ministry of Defense*

Counter-Adm. Radi A. Zubkov, *Committee of Scientists for Global Security*

CARNEGIE ENDOWMENT FOR INTERNATIONAL PEACE

The Carnegie Endowment for International Peace was established in 1910 in Washington, D.C., with a gift from Andrew Carnegie. As a tax-exempt operating (not grant-making) foundation, the Endowment conducts programs of research, discussion, publication, and education in international affairs and U.S. foreign policy. The Endowment publishes the quarterly magazine, *Foreign Policy*.

Carnegie's senior associates—whose backgrounds include government, journalism, law, academia, and public affairs—bring to their work substantial first-hand experience in foreign policy. Through writing, public and media appearances, study groups, and conferences, Carnegie associates seek to invigorate and extend both expert and public discussion on a wide range of international issues, including worldwide migration, nuclear nonproliferation, regional conflicts, multilateralism, democracy-building, and the use of force. The Endowment also engages in and encourages projects designed to foster innovative contributions in international affairs.

In 1993, the Carnegie Endowment committed its resources to the establishment of a public policy research center in Moscow designed to promote intellectual collaboration among scholars and specialists in the United States, Russia, and other post-Soviet states. Together with the Endowment's associates in Washington, the center's staff of Russian and American specialists conduct programs on a broad range of major policy issues ranging from economic reform to civil-military relations. The Carnegie Moscow Center holds seminars, workshops, and study groups at which international participants from academia, government, journalism, the private sector, and nongovernmental institutions gather to exchange views. It also provides a forum for prominent international figures to present their views to informed Moscow audiences. Associates of the center also host seminars in Kiev on an equally broad set of topics.

The Endowment normally does not take institutional positions on public policy issues. It supports its activities principally from its own resources, supplemented by nongovernmental, philanthropic grants.

Carnegie Endowment
for International Peace
1779 Massachusetts Ave., N.W.
Washington, D.C. 20036
Tel: 202-483-7600
Fax: 202-483-1840
e-mail: carnegie@ceip.org
Web Page: www.ceip.org

Carnegie Moscow Center
Ul. Tverskaya 16/2
7th Floor
Moscow 103009
Tel: 7-095-935-8904
Fax: 7-095-935-8906
e-mail: info@carnegie.ru
Web Page: www.carnegie.ru

www.ingramcontent.com/pod-product-compliance
Lightning Source LLC
Chambersburg PA
CBHW011829020426
42334CB00027B/2995